THE STORY OF MY LIFE

Books by
OSWALD J. SMITH

Messages on Salvation
THE COUNTRY I LOVE BEST
THE MARVELS OF GRACE

Messages on the Deeper Life
THE MAN GOD USES
THE ENDUEMENT OF POWER

Messages on Missions
THE CRY OF THE WORLD
TALES OF THE MISSION FIELD

Messages on Prophecy
PROPHECY—WHAT LIES AHEAD?

*Messages on Revival and
    Evangelism*
THE PASSION FOR SOULS

Messages on Special Subjects
THE CHALLENGE OF LIFE

Messages in Biography
THE LIVES OF BRAINERD AND
    FLETCHER
THE STORY OF MY LIFE

Messages for Young People
THE ADVENTURES OF ANDY
    MCGINNIS
THE STORIES OF THOMAS

Messages in Poetry
POEMS OF A LIFETIME

Messages in Hymns
OSWALD SMITH'S BEST SONGS
OSWALD SMITH'S FAVOURITES

*Dr. Oswald J. Smith has reduced the number of his books. Above is a
complete list of titles to be kept in circulation. All other titles have
been discontinued. The author has taken out some chapters from the
earlier editions of the books which will be continued under their former
titles and substituted some chapters from the books no longer in print.
In this way he has retained the most important material in a reduced
number of books.*

THE STORY OF
MY LIFE
AND THE PEOPLES CHURCH

by
OSWALD J. SMITH, Litt.D.

Founder of The Peoples Church, Toronto

Foreword by
REDD HARPER

MARSHALL, MORGAN & SCOTT
London

MARSHALL, MORGAN & SCOTT, LTD.
BLUNDELL HOUSE
GOODWOOD ROAD
LONDON S.E.14

AUSTRALIA
119 BURWOOD ROAD
MELBOURNE, E.13

NEW ZEALAND
3 CAMPBELL ROAD, BOX 24053
ROYAL OAK, AUCKLAND

SOUTH AFRICA
33 CENTRAL AVENUE, BOX 17
PINELANDS
CAPE

CANADA
HOME EVANGEL BOOKS LTD.
25 HOBSON AVENUE
TORONTO 16
ONTARIO

THE PEOPLES CHURCH, TORONTO
374 SHEPPARD AVE. EAST
WILLOWDALE
ONTARIO

SBN 551 05340 2
MADE AND PRINTED IN GREAT BRITAIN BY PURNELL AND SONS, LTD.
PAULTON (SOMERSET) AND LONDON

GOD CHOSE A COUNTRY LAD

To my Father on the occasion of the Golden Jubilee
of his Ministry—1908 to 1958.

My father was a country lad,
  His body weak and frail;
He used to trudge barefoot to school,
  With pet crow and lunch pail.

And no one ever thought that he
  Would live to be a man;
But God had work for him to do
  And for his life a plan.

Upon this blonde-haired, blue-eyed boy,
  Rich talents He bestowed;
He took him from the country lanes
  To walk another road.

Away from relatives and friends
  God led him by his hand;
And like disciples long ago
  He heeded His command.

Like Peter, James and John of old,
  Left all to follow Him;
In faith my father followed on,
  Though oft the path grew dim.

Because he listened to God's voice,
  Obeyed His first command,
He chose to send this country boy
  To ev'ry foreign land.

GOD CHOSE A COUNTRY LAD

And many others father sent
  To those who never heard,
Who never read of Jesus' love
  In God's own Holy Word.

And from his pen rich hymns of praise
  Have reached most ev'ry tongue;
Around this great wide world of ours
  His songs are played and sung.

His books have spread o'er all the earth,
  They've helped both young and old;
Until we reach the Glory Land
  Their worth will not be told.

Why didn't God choose someone strong?
  You may be prone to ask;
Because He looks upon the heart
  And fits men for the task.

He chose a little shepherd boy
  To fight a giant strong;
Thus showed His pow'r the greater far
  To all the doubting throng.

My father, like Enoch of old,
  Walked daily with his Lord;
And as he worshipped at His throne
  God saw his heart outpoured.

God saw that he would faithful be,
  On him he could depend;
He's preached God's Word for fifty years,
  He'll preach it to the end.

HOPE EVANGELINE

ABOUT THE AUTHOR

Dr. Oswald J. Smith was ordained a Presbyterian Minister. He is now the Minister of Missions of The Peoples Church, Toronto, which he founded forty years ago, and which today has an enrolment of 3,500. In 1958 he celebrated the Golden Jubilee of his ministry—1908 to 1958—fifty years of preaching, and in 1968 his Diamond Jubilee.

For nearly forty years, The Peoples Church has had the largest Sunday evening audience of any church in Canada, and now the largest Sunday School.

As an Evangelist, he has preached in Spurgeon's Tabernacle and Westminster Chapel, London; the Moody Church, Chicago, Park St. Church and Tremont Temple, Boston, the Church of the Open Door, Los Angeles, and other centres in Great Britain, the United States, South Africa, South America, Australia, New Zealand and the Orient.

As a Missionary Statesman, he has led his Church in a programme that has netted over six million dollars for Missions and is contributing over $300,000 each year towards the support of some 350 missionaries. "The Church Herald" speaks of him as "the Pastor of the leading Missionary Church on the face of the globe". Dr. Harold J. Ockenga says: "A greater impetus has been given to Missions by Dr. Oswald J. Smith than by any other living person."

As an Author, he has written 35 books, which have had a circulation of nearly three million copies in sixty different languages.

As a Poet and Hymn-Writer, he has written 1,200 hymns, poems and gospel songs, including such world-famous numbers as "Then Jesus Came", "God Understands", "The Glory of His Presence", "The Song of the Soul Set Free", "Saved", "Deeper and Deeper". Homer Rodeheaver spoke of him as "the greatest living hymn-writer in the world today".

As an Editor, he has published a magazine for over 47 years, which enjoys a worldwide circulation.

As a World-Traveller, he has seen 72 countries.

The Fleming H. Revell Co. says of him: "There is a fire in his bones. Those who have heard him have seen fire in his heart, his eyes, his speech—a fire which has leaped out to set them afire. He has started in our world a great blaze of hope."

Billy Graham writes: "The name, Oswald J. Smith, symbolizes worldwide evangelization. His books have been used of the Holy Spirit to sear into the very depths of my soul and have had a tremendous influence on my personal life and ministry."

1968   —The Press.

THE FULFILMENT OF A VISION

The Peoples Church originated from a God-given vision received by Oswald J. Smith when he was praying and fasting with Dr. E. Ralph Hooper on the trunk of a fallen tree across a gully in the wilds of British Columbia on July 11, 1919 as recorded in chapter seven.

Returning to Toronto, he launched The Gospel Auditorium on October 3, 1920. After that the work passed through several phases. For instance, there was the Parkdale Tabernacle, Massey Hall, the Tent, the Alliance Tabernacle, The Cosmopolitan Tabernacle, the Toronto Gospel Tabernacle, and finally, The Peoples Church.

Hence, The Peoples Church really started some 48 years ago. The present pastor is Rev. Paul B. Smith, B.A., D.D., the youngest son of the Founder. Dr. Oswald J. Smith is still the Minister of Missions and is as active as ever.

Thus the vision received on July 11, 1919, passed through many phases before it was finally fulfilled. It is a long, and fascinating story of God's guidance down through the years. How wonderful are His ways!

FOREWORD

I HAVE just taken the most exciting journey of my life—a journey filled with danger and suspense, mystery and courage, love and adventure, defeat and triumph, tears and joy! A journey that not only thrilled and inspired my heart but gave me courage to ". . . press toward the mark for the prize of the high calling of God in Christ Jesus". You, dear reader, are about to take this same journey!

And as you walk alongside of Oswald J. Smith in this—the story of his life and ministry—I know that you, too, will be thrilled and challenged as never before. Not only by his completely consecrated life but also by this concrete example of the manifestation of the Power of God.

I shall never forget the first time I heard Dr. Smith speak. It was at Forest Home in the summer of 1951 when I was scarcely a year old in the Lord. The first person I met on arrival was Cindy Walker. (You will recall Cindy as the girl who played my sister in the film "Mr. Texas".) The first thing Cindy said to me was, "Dr. Smith will give you something worth while." Cindy was right. Dr. Smith through the power of the Holy Spirit DID give me many things worth while.

Dr. Smith also gave me several of his books. These proved to be about the first books I had read as a "babe in Christ" which really spoke to my heart and drew me closer to The Master. In fact, his "THE ENDUEMENT OF POWER" and "THE MAN GOD USES" so spoke to my heart that in a few months I completely surrendered my life to Christ for full time service. And if you have not read these two books I urge you to do so right away.

I was more than surprised a few weeks later when upon arrival at the Curtis Hotel in Minneapolis there was a letter awaiting me from Dr. Oswald J. Smith. Having spent less than an hour with him personally at the conference, just to hear from him was surprise enough, but the contents of the letter actually flabbergasted me.

Enclosed were several of his hymn lyrics and a letter asking me to compose music for them. I just could hardly believe this great hymn-writer who had written so many well known hymns with all the great writers of the day, would ask me—a babe in Christ and strictly a cowboy musician—to compose music for his lyrics. I knelt right then and there by my bed and thanked my Redeemer for being so good to me and told Him if He wished to send me a melody for any of the lyrics by Dr. Smith—I was available. Before I left that room, God had answered that prayer and sent me a beautiful melody for one of the poems.

From that day to this, the Lord has been most gracious to us and we have now written together 15 Gospel songs, all of which have been recorded. Our latest—COME WITH YOUR HEARTACHE—looks at present to be the biggest. Already recorded and featured by George Beverly Shea in the Billy Graham meetings and on the Hour of Decision radio broadcasts, it has been published in the U.S.A., Canada and Great Britain.

Yes, I feel sure that as you read this exciting book and take this very eventful journey as I did through many, many lands and actually live these true-life experiences with Oswald J. Smith, you too will be inspired as I and countless others have been by the sheer force of his personality and Christlike life. But more than that, you will come to know why he is known throughout the world as the "Elder Statesman of Christendom".

PLEASE . . . read this book slowly. Do not miss a single word. Live this wonderful life with him every moment. And as you journey along with him from those simple beginnings in that little country station over every kind of terrain, by every known mode of transportation from horseback to modern jet planes to almost every known corner of this old globe and then safely back again into the great Peoples Church of Toronto, I will be praying that God in His infinite mercy and grace will give to many of you a similar vision, challenge and commission to *"Go into all the world, and preach the gospel to every creature"*.

Hollywood, Calif.   REDD HARPER.

CONTENTS

THE GLORY OF HIS PRESENCE

Rev. Oswald J. Smith

B. D. Ackley

SOLO

1. I have walked a - lone with Je - sus In a fel - low - ship di - vine;
2. On the moun - tain I have seen Him, Christ my Com - fort - er and Friend;
3. In my fail - ure, sin and sor - row, Bro - ken - heart - ed, crushed and torn,
4. In the dark - ness, in the shad - ow. With the Sav - ior I have trod,

Nev - er - more can earth al - lure me, I am His and He is mine.
And the glo - ry of that vi - sion Will be with me to the end.
I have felt His pres - ence near me, He has all my bur - dens borne.
Sweet in - deed have been the les - sons, Since I've walked a - lone with God.

CHORUS

I have seen Him, I have known Him, For He deigns to walk with me; And the glory of His

pres - ence will be mine e - ter - nal - ly. O the glo - ry of His pres - ence, O the

beau - ty of His face; I am His and His for - ev - er, He has won me by His grace.

CHAPTER I

BOYHOOD DAYS

THREE times in the New Testament the Spirit of God relates the story of Paul's conversion, for oftentimes personal testimony makes a greater appeal than preaching. I offer no apologies therefore for telling the story of what God has done for me.

My father was born in Sherbrooke, Quebec, December 18th, 1862, and my mother at Ernestown, Ontario, December 5th, 1868. They were married in Odessa on December 5th, 1887.

I was born in a farmhouse on the outskirts of Odessa, Ontario, November 8th, 1889, and I am the eldest of ten, four girls and six boys. My father was a telegraph operator, hence my childhood days were spent in railway stations, my babyhood at Elmstead, Walkerville and Woodstock, and my boyhood at Embro, a country station on the C.P.R., four miles from the village.

Night after night the trains thundered by my bedroom window, but I seldom heard them. The spot where the station stood is now a ploughed field, the building in which we lived for thirteen years having been moved a mile west, and the name changed to Zorra. Our nearest village, Beachville, was three and a half miles away. Woodstock was six miles east of us, and London twenty miles west.

We arrived at Embro on July 1st, 1893, and left on July 1st, 1906. After a few months in Toronto, my father was sent to open the C.N.R. station at Mount Albert on October 16th, 1906. Our family moved to Toronto on May 1st, 1913, and lived at 802 Logan Avenue.

I can never pass the old Embro Station (Zorra) without a lump in my throat. Many a time during these later years, in travelling to Chicago and California to hold campaigns, I have had to pass by it. Always I have gazed eagerly over the landscape on either side. I know every road and path, every field and wood, every farmhouse and the spot where the old freight shed stood. The very ground is sacred to me, for it was the scene of my childhood days, where as a boy I roved, barefooted; and to me it is home.

My father had many qualities of culture and refinement. He was most kind and indulgent, and always gracious and courteous in his dealings with the public. As he grew older, he became more contented and patient; seldom, if ever, was he known to complain. He played the violin by ear a little and loved to play it. He was a master at checkers; all that I know about the game I learned from him. He never stood in my way.

My mother, whose disposition was always bright and optimistic, was active, energetic and wholly devoted to her large family. No sacrifice was too great, no task too hard, for her willing heart and hands. Her work was hard and her hours long. Only God knows the number of nights she walked the floor, rocked the cradle, or sat by the bedside of her children during their many, many ailments. Separated from loved ones, dwelling among strangers, making the best of a railway station for a home, four miles from a doctor, her lot was not an enviable one. But there is One Who has bottled up her tears and will accord her a rich reward.

DELICATE IN HEALTH

I was delicate, thin and tall, and not able to take my own part. Hence my early school days hold many unpleasant memories. We were compelled to walk a mile and a half to the little country school-house at Cody's Corners, summer and winter alike.

My first teacher was an elderly man, Mr. H. C. Ross. He was followed by Billy Blair, who later discovered a rich mine in Northern Ontario and became wealthy. My third teacher was Lottie Nethercott, to whom I went for five years and who later married Billy Blair. She meant the most to me. My last teacher was Miss Winters, who married a Mr. Ward. It was for Miss Nethercott I wrote my first poem when I was only fifteen. It closed with these lines:

> "We'll talk when old men of the past,
> Of the days at Cody's Corners
> And the teacher we loved so well."

At one time I passed through a severe illness of pneumonia, and upon several occasions while at school or play I fainted dead away. Well do I recall a neighbour one day saying to another when I was supposed to be out of ear-shot—"Well, poor boy, he's not long for this world." And thus I was comforted. Many never expected me to reach manhood. While standing in class one morning, suddenly all grew dark, and the back of my head came into violent contact with the floor. After I came to, I was put on the stage coach, driven by Mr. William Vannatter, and taken home, hence to remain for two years out of school. My teacher said, "That boy will never live to see a mission field." Rev. C. Hayengar wrote: "He hasn't many more days on this earth."

But in spite of my weakness I did grow up; I did reach manhood, and God has allowed me to preach the Gospel throughout the world.

MEMORIES OF THE PAST

One night I was scared out of my wits by a tramp in a barn. Later the station was robbed while we slept, and for a while excitement ran high. A boy from Embro Village once gave me a black eye on the way home from school. Many a time we visited the old swimming hole and the river where we learned to swim long before we had ever heard of bathing suits. Once we had a pet crow that could talk. Tommy would follow us to school and home again. One day I rode a steer with long horns and was heavily thrown to the ground. Ernie and I raised hundreds of rabbits and white rats, and some pigeons, with which we spent many happy hours, but for which the farmers never forgave us. There were bitter cold days when we had to trudge to school through deep snow. Many a skating party did we have on the country ice. Hours we spent playing in the old freight shed. When the doctor tried to snare out my tonsils the wire stuck.

For several summers we played "house" under the old walnut tree. We often went hunting in the woods. In the spring there was the boiling of the maple sap out under the trees. We had a pony named Queenie, and she had a colt named Prince. We had a Great Dane with a broken leg and his daughter Fawn. At one time our station was moved across the tracks while we were living in it. We watched with great interest the erection and testing of one of the world's first wig-wags at our crossing. There was a time when mother was seriously ill with rheumatism, and Ernie and I had to be taken on a bob-sleigh through the snow to stay at Mrs. Nichol's. On July 5th, 1893, the Zorra Tug-of-War Team won the world championship at Chicago. Nor will I forget the school concert when my teacher, Miss Winters, chose "Goodbye, My Blue-bell" for me to sing as a solo. These are some of the memories that still linger of my boyhood days.

I lived in the horse and buggy days. There were no auto-mobiles when I was a boy and no paved highways; there were no radios or television sets, and no aeroplanes. I saw them all come in. City streets were built of wooden blocks. The side-walks were board. Gas lamps provided what light there was. Horse cars were just passing out, electric light was beginning to be used in the cities, and telephones were being installed. I lived in the Victorian age and the new had not yet been born.

On July 23rd, 1905, our home was saddened and the family tie broken by the death of my eldest sister, Hazel. It made a deep impression on me. She was only ten years of age when she died. Her tombstone may be seen in the Embro cemetery today, one mile north of the village.

It has never been my policy to look for a position or to sit down and wait for a call. Always I have created my own work, and generally work for others as well. Even in my boyhood days I endeavoured to earn and save. First of all my brother and I got two settings of eggs and borrowed a couple of hens. With the money we saved from the sale of eggs we bought a cow. We sold milk and got two pigs. Now and again we weighed cattle and bedded cars, sawed wood, carried coal, lit lamps, hoed corn and did other odd jobs. Thus we earned what we could and saved practically all, until, when finally I left home for good at the age of seventeen, I had saved up about eighty dollars, with which to start life. Money was scarce when I was young and it was hard to get. Hoeing corn brought me 25 cents for a whole afternoon's work in the hot sun. Milk brought us five cents a quart and eggs eight cents a dozen. Men earned a dollar a day. My father, $35.00 a month.

As far back as I can remember I was of a religious disposi-tion. I seldom neglected prayer at night. I recall asking mother about forgiveness, telling my brother, Ernie, when quite young, to prepare for Heaven, of being very much afraid of swearing, lying, etc. And yet I had no knowledge of salvation. I recall very indistinctly the inside of a church. My mother was a Christian, but I knew nothing of conversion. My ground for salvation was works. Later, father too trusted Christ. I had prayed for him every day for 47 years.

As a boy I took pleasure in climbing up and crawling along the eaves on the roof of the station. I used to reason it out this way: "If I should lose my balance and fall some day, all I would have to do would be to offer a prayer for pardon before I crashed to the ground and I would be forgiven for the last sins I had committed." I did not then know anything about the cleansing blood that continually cleanses from sin as we walk in the light.

THE OLD DITCH DIGGER

There came a time when something happened in our community that had a tremendous influence on my life. There was an old ditch digger, Richardson by name, who was an inveterate drunkard. He had a large red nose full of holes which had developed as a result of his heavy drinking. One day this man was gloriously saved.

He started holding cottage meetings in the homes of the farmers round about the railway station, and many a meeting found me there. There was something in my young heart that cried out for these gatherings. Alone I would leave my father's station and trudge along the country road under the starlit sky to the house where the prayer meeting was to be held, and sit there spellbound.

Then one day he came and asked my father for permission to hold meetings in the waiting room of the station, to which my father gave his consent. After that I did not have to go to the meetings, the meetings had come to me. Every Sunday night I attended, and listened to the old ditch digger as he led the people in the singing of gospel hymns and proclaimed the story of redemption. There was an atmosphere about those meetings that I have never forgotten, yet I did not get converted.

Then one night I was tremendously influenced by Herb Sykes, a wicked orphan boy whom God had gloriously saved. He held a gospel service in the school-house which I have never forgotten. He sang the new gospel song, "Count Your Many

Blessings." It was the first time I had ever heard it. Someone tried to disturb the meeting, and Dan Parsons threatened to fight him.

"I WILL BE THAT BOY"

July and August are hot months in Canada, and the farmers are busy, but they found time in our community to conduct a Sunday School in the little brick school-house at Cody's Corners. My brother and I used to walk along the country road, one and a half miles, to this Sunday School.

One day our teacher, the daughter of a farmer, Grace Featherson by name, turned to us and said: "Any one of you boys might be a minister." I do not know what happened in the hearts of the other boys but I answered immediately, "I will be that boy." From that day to the day I preached my first sermon I never had a desire to do anything else, though I was not even saved. That was a crisis hour in my life.

When I was twelve I was fascinated and tremendously influenced by slides on the Pilgrim's Progress, given by Miss Isabel McIntosh, a deeply spiritual Presbyterian missionary, in St. Mark's Church, Toronto, later called Dale, where, years after, I became pastor. She was the first to ask me definitely if I had been saved.

CONVERTED AT LAST

When I was sixteen years of age, in the year 1906, the greatest event of my life took place. The newspapers were brought on the train from Toronto. The section men would open them up quickly and sit on the benches, reading the news of the day.

At this time the papers contained startling news. We commenced to read of a great evangelistic campaign that was being conducted by Dr. R. A. Torrey and Mr. Chas. M. Alexander, preacher and singer, and we read that the whole city of Toronto was stirred; that some were coming in from 200 miles around; that the meetings were attended by 3,400 people; that the hall was packed in a few minutes, and that multiplied hundreds were unable to gain admission.

I had never before heard of an evangelist. I had never been to an evangelistic campaign in my life. I was an ignorant country boy, but something in my heart led me to read those newspaper reports. Dr. Torrey's addresses were published word for word, column after column, day by day, and Mr. Alexander's hymns, especially "The Glory Song", were reproduced, both words and music.

From time to time mother would say: "So and so is under conviction," as the section men and farmers read the accounts. As for me, I did not know the meaning of the word "conviction" or "conversion", but day by day my interest grew as the papers continued to bring news of the campaign.

At last, strangely moved, my brother Ernie and I asked mother if we might go to Toronto to attend the meetings, and she wisely gave her permission. I often wonder what would have happened had she refused. Toronto was ninety-four miles away.

It was a great day when we left the old Embro station and boarded the train for the distant city. We went to the home of our Aunt Phoebe (Mrs. Thos. Findley). Immediately we inquired the way to Massey Hall. We got on a Yonge Street car and when we got off at Shuter Street and went around behind the car, we saw something that arrested our attention at once —a large crowd of people. Hurrying forward we saw that they were standing before the great doors of Massey Hall waiting for them to open. Being boys we elbowed our way through to the front. Half an hour later the doors opened, and we were almost lifted up in the press, and carried into the Hall. I looked around in amazement, for I had only been accustomed to a little country school-house before. I gazed at the immense hall, at the first and second galleries right around the building, in a sort of a dazed condition. It was all so new to me. But people were pouring in and so we hurried to get a seat. In ten minutes the auditorium was packed, and hundreds were turned away.

We had arrived in time for the last eight meetings, and never missed one. Why others did not go who lived right in the city I could not understand, for we had travelled nearly one hundred miles to be present. Never will I forget those meetings. Everything was new and strange. I was fascinated. My eyes were filled with wonder and amazement. Never had I beheld such a scene before. I did not miss a single service. Moreover I was never shut out for I always got there on time and always got a seat.

I sat for a while gazing around. Presently I saw a man with a smiling face step out on the platform. He commenced to wave his arms. I had never seen a man do that before. The audience was singing "The Glory Song", and I was carried up into the realms of Heaven. Oh what singing! I am used to it now, but how it thrilled me then. I soon realized of course that for the first time in my life I was looking at the world's greatest song leader, Charles M. Alexander. So filled with curiosity was I that I sat with my ears, mouth and eyes wide open. Robert Harkness of Australia was the pianist.

The second to last meeting came. We had made up our minds to accept Christ that afternoon. It was a special service for boys. There were 3,400 present. We did not know then that our mother had written to Dr. Torrey asking him to pray that her sons might be converted. We arrived early and the Hall was crowded. What Dr. Torrey said I do not remember. But I will never forget the way he repeated his text, Isaiah 53 : 5—"But He was wounded for *my* transgressions; He was bruised for *my* iniquities, the chastisement of *my* peace was upon Him, and with His stripes *I* am healed."

At the close of his message he asked those 25 and over who wanted to accept Christ to come forward. Some responded. Little by little he lowered the ages until I was included. But to my amazement I was turned into a chunk of lead. I could not move. I did not know then about the power of Satan, but I have found out since. Presently my brother quietly nudged me, and that broke the spell. I sprang out of my seat and with a sober face I took the momentous step. For a moment I found myself alone at the front, then I grasped Dr. Torrey's hand and went down into the inquiry room in the basement where I sat on a chair. A man came and spoke to me and then left. But I saw no light and got nowhere, though he thought I was through.

Then suddenly it happened. I cannot explain it even today. I just bowed my head, put my face between my hands and in a moment the tears gushed through my fingers, and fell on the chair, and there stole into my boyish heart a realization of the fact that the great change had taken place. Christ had entered and I was a new creature. I had been born again. There was no excitement, no unusual feeling, but I knew that something had happened, and that ever after all life would be different. That was on January 28th, 1906, when I was 16 years of age, and it has lasted to this day. Yes, and it is going to last, praise God, throughout the countless ages of eternity.

Scores of others came, Ernie among them. He is now (Rev. E. Gilmour Smith, B.A., D.D.) a minister in the United Church of Canada.

HOME AGAIN

Upon returning home I was very backward in confessing Christ though I did speak to some of the boys at school. They all knew that I had become a Christian. But oh, how my young heart yearned to do some definite work for God. Here I was with no church, no pastor, no fellowship—a raw, country boy, standing practically alone for God. But I did not backslide. I believe you can put a true born-again convert anywhere and he will be kept by the power of God. My one petition was, "Lord, what wilt Thou have me to do?" I cannot understand a man professing to be saved and not wanting to do something for the Lord Jesus.

Day after day I went to my room and pored over the pages of the Bible. Night after night as I knelt in prayer I cried to God to make me an evangelist, for I had seen a vision. I had just come from the great meetings in Massey Hall. But I did not know how to become an evangelist. I did not know that a Seminary course is necessary. I only knew that I wanted to preach. Finally with mother's help I started a Sunday School in my own home and gathered in the neighbour's children. Many a time as I walked on the railway tracks to light the semaphore lamp, I sang and preached to the birds and trees in my joy, as I thought of and longed for Christian service. How well do I remember singing at the top of my voice, as I walked the railway ties, the song I had heard sung in Massey Hall: "I am so Glad that Jesus Loves Me." And no one ever interrupted me or told me that I was too long, so I preached and sang to my heart's content. I made up sermons in bed at night and imagined I was preaching them to crowds of people.

After leaving Embro and while living in Toronto, I worked in the office of Massey-Harris at a salary of $3.00 per week. Later, my uncle, Thomas Findley, became president of the firm.

During this time I came into touch with the Hornorites, and for several months I doubted my salvation. Night after night I went forward in the tent, regardless of the crowds, and knelt in the straw, where I cried to God to save me, the workers gathering around and praying together. Thus I was seeking salvation by experience and feeling rather than through faith in Christ. It was a sad delusion and led me into great darkness. Oh, how I suffered! "Am I saved or am I lost?" This was my question day and night. At last I got hold of that priceless little pamphlet, "Safety, Certainty and Enjoyment", and peace returned.

One day while in Massey-Harris, I fainted. I was taken home and accompanied the family to Mount Albert, where I became very ill. At last I recovered and attended High School for a few months, but finally returned to Toronto to work under Mr. Herbert Daly, a second cousin, in the office of the National Cash Register Co., on Lombard St., at a salary of $8.00 per week. I remained for one full year, and saved between $3.00 and $4.00 a week. I had now, at the age of seventeen, left home for good.

CALLED TO PREACH

At both Embro and Mt. Albert my desire to preach had grown stronger day by day. I felt as though I could not wait for the time to come. So desperate was I that I made a very special plan. I said to myself, "I will go far away from home. I will go so far away that no one will know me. I will go ten miles away, at least. And I will find a little country church and ask the minister to let me preach, and if I fail I will then know that I am not called, and will return home a wiser boy."

You see, I had no one to advise me, no one to tell me what to do. How to get into the ministry was the question. I had to make a start, a beginning. I knew within myself that I could preach. I felt it in my very bones, and my whole soul cried out for an opportunity to put myself on trial. But I did not have to carry out my plan. One day the Presbyterian minister of Mt. Albert, Rev. D. G. Cameron, asked me if I would say a few words to the Young People's Society. He did not have to ask twice. Later I went to the city of Toronto and spoke briefly on missionary work in Japan (which incidentally, I knew nothing about) to a Young People's Society in Beverley Street Baptist Church.

"God moves in a mysterious way His wonders to perform." I was in my humble little room (2 Bruce St.) when, one day, I glanced at an old copy of The Presbyterian, and saw a brief announcement about the Toronto Bible College, which resulted in my attending the Evening Classes for one term. Oh, how my heart rejoiced as I made my way twice a week to that sacred hall. To me it was the very gate of Heaven, and became the outlet for my pent-up energies in several fields of happy service. I taught in Central Prison, helped in The King's Mission, Yonge St. Mission, The House of Refuge, etc. Some professed conversion in the Prison. I attended Beverley St. Baptist Church, of which Rev. Wm. Wallace was the pastor, and assisted in a Bible Study for boys. I was then eighteen. A new world had opened up to me.

At first I joined Chalmers Presbyterian Church. But one day I heard two or three discussing a new minister whom they said was now pastor of St. Mark's Church and was doing a unique work, and I decided to go and hear him. Rev. J. D. Morrow was his name. When he took charge the attendance was about thirty each Sunday. Within eight months, he had some two hundred members, mostly from the working classes.

Never will I forget that first night. The church was full. He preached from the text: "The harvest is past, the summer is ended, and we are not saved" (Jer. 8: 20). Oh, how he pled! There was life in every word. The service was evangelistic and I became a captive at once.

Little did the preacher know as he spoke, that his future Associate Pastor and successor was listening to him that night, that his every action stirred the heart of a young man only eighteen, as he had not been moved since the great Massey Hall meetings of two years before. I at once asked for a Sunday School class and was given a group of small girls to teach. I have never waited to be asked to do something: so anxious have I been for Christian work that it has always been my policy to seek it. Thus I came into contact with Mr. Morrow, whom I tremendously admired. I immediately joined St. Mark's Presbyterian Church.

At the end of the term in the Bible College I applied for a mission field under the Presbyterian Church. I remember even now how Mr. Morrow pled with the Committee in Old St. James, where I later became Pastor, to accept me; but they considered me too young and refused. Then I applied to the Upper Canada Bible Society and was sent by Rev. Jesse Gibson as a colporteur to Muskoka, where I sold Bibles during the summer of 1908. It was a rich experience and taught me how to endure hardships for the Lord Jesus. Sometimes the door

was slammed in my face. I was again and again refused food
and shelter, and once had to sleep outdoors in a barley field.

MY DREAMS COME TRUE

But now at last came the opportunity for which I had prayed
and waited so long. One day I got off the train at a little wayside station called Severn. I waited, watching the people
depart, until there was only one man left. He stepped up to
me and asked me my business. I told him. Then he said, "I
am the Methodist minister; you had better come home with
me." He was the Rev. Elijah Brown.

As we started towards his home, he suddenly paused.
"Would you mind preaching for me tomorrow?" he asked.
Would I mind! That was what I had been living for. That
had been my dream night and day. I did not give him a
chance to change his mind. "Yes," I cried, "I will be glad to
preach for you." Then fearing he might ask if I had preached
before, since I was so young, I fell behind. Had he asked that
question, I thought, the sun would have fallen from my sky.
But sure enough, he did, and in a moment my heart was in my
mouth. "I suppose you have spoken before?" he inquired.
The very question I had dreaded. How would I answer? I
could not bear to miss the opportunity. Suddenly, like a
drowning man grasping at a straw, I grasped at the word
"spoken". "Oh yes," I replied, "I have *spoken* before." Twice
I had given brief messages at Young People's meetings. My
answer seemed to satisfy him, for he said no more about it.
Then he said something that almost took my breath. "I have
three appointments; will you preach at all three?" "Yes," I
exclaimed, "gladly!" And my young heart throbbed with
joy.

In a corner of my room that night I knelt in prayer with my
forehead touching the floor, and pled for guidance. I did not
have a sermon for I had forgotten every one I had made up in
bed. What was I to say? I remembered listening to a sermon
in Toronto in Beverley Street Baptist Church by the Rev.
Elmore Harris, D.D., one of the editors of the Scofield Reference Bible, on Ephesians 1: 3, a text that no one should take
until he has been in the ministry 25 years at least, and since I
had a good memory I was able to recall much of what I had
heard. So I decided to use it. How my soul was thrilled as I

thought of the morrow and its tremendous possibilities. My dreams and visions were at last to be fulfilled. I would now know whether or not I could preach. My hour had come. Rising from my knees I went to bed, turned out the light and slept like a child.

MY FIRST SUNDAY IN THE PULPIT

Well, the morning came and I preached in Severn, and for at least thirty minutes I spoke without a pause, without a note, nor did my memory fail me once. There I stood, picturing Dr. Harris in my mind's eye, recalling all I could of what he had said, and passing it out to the people before me. How it sounded, or what they thought I do not know. I had preached, that was sufficient, and I left praising God for His vindication. I had found myself at last.

That afternoon we drove to the country church at Wesley, and as we were driving along the minister commenced to talk to me about Calvinism and Arminianism. I had never heard of Calvinism and Arminianism before, and all I could say was, "Yes, I suppose so. I think so." Then he said, "You know, I think we Methodists have the better of it." I could only say, "Yes, I think you have," and all the time I was praying to God for another sermon. "Lord," I said, "I cannot preach the same sermon I did this morning, or this minister will think it is all I have. I must have another." Then the Serpent in the Wilderness came to my mind. I decided to take as my text John 3: 14-15, and trust God to see me through.

The minister introduced me and the service commenced. But right in the middle of the sermon I heard the sound of a train, and I knew I would have to do one of two things—either keep going and let the people lose what I said, or stop till the train passed, as it went right by the church. Finally, I decided it was too dangerous to stop, for I might never get started again, so I decided to keep going while the going was good! As the train thundered by, the people saw that I was speaking by the movement of my lips, but of course they could not hear a word. There were smiles, but I was still going strong when the train had passed!

Before I went to the evening service at Washago, the largest place of all, I said, "Lord, I will have to have sermon number three, or he will think I have only two sermons." The Parable

of the Ten Virgins came to my mind, and I decided to use
that. When the minister rose to introduce me, he said, "I have
received a great blessing from the preaching of our young
brother today." I was quite taken back. All I had been asking
was, "Can I keep going?" I had not thought about blessing.
Finally, I gave my message, speaking for about forty minutes,
and sat down.

How happy I was that night as we drove back to Severn
under the starlit sky! I knew now that God had called me to
preach. I was walking on air, and from that day to this I have
preached somewhere in the world every year of my life.
Whereas I went as an ignorant country boy to the great
Massey Hall, later I used that same hall for my church, and I,
too, looked out at those two great galleries filled with people,
and had the joy of telling out the Gospel as Dr. Torrey did
before me. Wondrous are the ways of the Lord!

Thus the year 1908 became a great and never to be forgotten
year in my life, for it was the year of the commencement of
my Ministry. It was the year that saw me in full time service
for God when I was only 18 years of age, a service that has
continued to this day. From that service I have never turned
back.

If I could go back to 1906, after having experienced the ups
and downs of the Christian life, I would do again exactly what
I did then ; I would again open my heart to the Lord Jesus and
accept Him as my personal Saviour. And if I could go back
to 1908, after having known the ups and downs of a minister's
life, I would again decide for the ministry of the Lord Jesus
Christ : I would give my life once more to the greatest work in
the world—the proclamation of the Gospel. If you, my friend,
have been called and have disobeyed, will you not now obey
God? And if you have not yet accepted Christ as your Saviour,
will you not do so now, before it is forever too late?

CHAPTER II

AMONG THE INDIANS

IT WAS in Mount Albert. I had just returned from my summer's work as colporteur. A telegram awaited me. It was from the Bible Society asking me if I would go to British Columbia and launch the work on the Pacific Coast. It seemed almost too good to be true. My work in Muskoka had been quite successful; hence I was chosen for British Columbia.

How lonely I was the night I boarded the tourist coach for my distant field. Never will I forget it. Ernie came to see me off. Three thousand miles of travel that would occupy some five or six days lay before me. I was only eighteen. It was September 10th, 1908. I cooked my own meals enroute.

Passing through Winnipeg, we crossed the great prairies of the West and at last reached the majestic Rockies. I will not stop to describe them. They filled me with wonder and awe, but I have been over them often since, as well as through the Swiss Alps, and space forbids the detailed description with which my diary abounds. Suffice it to say that at last we reached Vancouver and the train part of my journey was over.

After two days in Vancouver I secured my Bibles and boarded the *Camosun* for Prince Rupert. I had a most exciting voyage up the coast, getting my first view of open sea at Queen Charlotte Sound. The scenery of snow-clad mountains, hundreds of picturesque islands, etc., was most entrancing. The lower deck was filthy. It was thronged with Chinese, Hindoos, and numerous European nationalities travelling steerage. My accommodation was rough second-class. At last we reached Prince Rupert, the new terminal of the Canadian National Railway. There were but three streets, built on the tops of stumps, and about six hundred inhabitants. It was a desolate-looking place. Tents were everywhere.

STRANGE EXPERIENCES

We arrived at one o'clock Sunday morning, and at eleven and seven I preached for the Rev. C. Kidd in the canvas-covered Presbyterian Church. I visited nearly every home, sold a large number of Bibles, and received many rebuffs. I also called at the construction camps but met with little success.

Lack of space forbids me telling of my duck-hunting experience in an open boat, when, in failing to kill a wounded duck, I struck it with the end of the oar, killed the duck, but drove the oar right through the bottom of the boat. It was a narrow escape, and if there had not been a small island a quarter of a mile away to which I paddled while my partner held his big hand over the hole, we might have been drowned.

I left Prince Rupert for Port Essington on the steam tug *Native*. The day was dark. The rain was falling. The wind was high and a big sea running. I enjoyed the voyage greatly for it was my first experience on the ocean in a storm. The little tug struck the waters bravely, but rolled from side to side almost to the water's edge, climbed the great waves and bounded down head first, while the huge billows broke over her decks again and again.

Finally we covered the thirty miles and reached Port Essington, where I was kindly taken into the family of the Methodist missionary to the Indians, Rev. C. B. Freeman, to whom I owe a debt of gratitude. There was no place that seemed so much like home. Mrs. Freeman was like a mother to me. How often I thought of the dear ones three thousand miles away, as I joined their happy family circle. There were three girls and two boys, and I myself was but a boy of eighteen.

On Sunday I preached to the Indians in Mr. Freeman's church, and through the week had the joy of selling Bibles to them. And a real joy it was, for they welcomed me in every home and never once showed the rebellious spirit of the whites. I picked up a little of the Chinook or trade language of the Indians, which is understood by all. While among them I received a letter from the Rev. Thos. Crosby, the great veteran missionary to the Indians of the Pacific Coast, author of "Among the Ankomenums". He has now gone to his reward.

Arriving at Fort Simpson on the *Princess Beatrice*, the largest Indian village on the coast, I was entertained by

Captain George Roe of the Salvation Army, who showed me unusual kindness. It was a real joy to assist him in his lonely work. So eager were the Indians for Bibles that I sold out in five hours and was compelled to return to Port Essington for more.

Determined to do what I could for the construction men, I took the river boat up the Skeena to Copper River, a distance of one hundred miles. The railway had not then been laid. It was a lonely experience—the great forest filled with wild beasts, an Indian village, New Town, two miles away, and rough, godless men in the camps. At one time I missed the trail and wandered alone in the dense woods long after dark. In fact, I lost my way five times. I tremble now as I think of the bears that might have attacked me. I did not carry a gun. God Himself must have protected.

One day, after sunset, I left New Town, the Indian village, and started back to camp, but lost the trail before I had gone half a mile. After vainly attempting to find it, I made straight through the forest in the direction I thought the river would be found. Finally I struck it and followed the shore over rocks and brush, through the dark, dreary solitude of the great forest, with the ghost-like mountains looming up in the distance, until I came to a place where I thought I could again find the lost trail. Entering once more the dark woods, I searched for awhile and presently found it. At one spot I had to cross a small river on a dead tree about a foot wide. In the daytime I did not mind, but at night, with the dark water flowing beneath, I was nervous. But God protected, and at last I found my little cabin. Oh, how precious was the Saviour during that time!

I sold a large number of Bibles in the Indian village, but few in the camp. The river kept going down until I despaired of another boat coming up, and was just about to arrange with an Indian to take me down in his dug-out, when the steamer appeared and in a short time I was again at Port Essington.

From Port Essington I went to Hartley Bay, an Indian village, and sold many Bibles. At night I was very ill, but I prayed, and the answer came like a flash of lightning. At midnight I left on the *Venture,* took a deck passage, spread my blankets on some boards and went to sleep, but was disturbed from time to time by an insane Indian. Arriving at Bella Bella, I preached for Dr. Large, a medical missionary, sold many

Bibles to the Indians, and then boarded the *Camosun* for Alert
Bay. We were detained by a heavy fog and arrived at
midnight.

It gave me an uncanny feeling to pass by the great Indian
houses that once contained a dozen families, with huge, painted
totem poles in front of each, carved into the likeness of
animals, birds and men. Rev. and Mrs. Hall, the Anglican
missionaries, received me and showed me no little kindness.
They had spent most of their lives among the Indians. I sold
all my Bibles and returned to Port Essington on the *Venture*.
I was on board three nights, and I slept on the deck.

Finally, I reached Port Essington, having travelled one
thousand miles since leaving there, and immediately returned
to Fort Simpson. Here, Rev. G. H. Raley, the Methodist
missionary, appointed me to assist Mr. Dineen in the Boys'
Home, after my Bibles were sold. While there Mr. Raley's
home was burned to the ground, and, later, a store, which
hundreds of Indians tried to save, along with many other
buildings. I had the pleasure of preaching to the Indians
several times in Fort Simpson, and have seen as many as
seven hundred gathered in the large church. They are great
singers. I loved to hear them sing in their own language. Never
will I forget their rendering of the Hallelujah Chorus. They
are also good at leading gospel services and are natural-born
orators.

Christmas came at last, my first Christmas away from home.
The Indians had a Christmas tree and a Santa Claus. Gifts
were distributed, and everyone was happy. But oh, the home-
sickness, the longing for the dear ones far away!

HARTLEY BAY

Winter had now set in, and since it was impossible to carry
on my colportage work, I accepted Mr. Raley's appointment
as missionary to the Indians of Hartley Bay.

I bought about twenty dollars' worth of food, a small cook
stove, an axe, hammer and nails, two quilts and a blanket. I
had fifteen jars of fruit and jelly donated to me. Boarding the
Princess May, I arrived at Hartley Bay once more and found
the village almost hidden in the deep snow. I was greeted by
a group of Indians and at once made my way to the mission
house, but so deep was the snow that I could only get as far

as the church. Taking a shovel, I began to clear the path to my future home. The snow was fully five feet deep.

It would be impossible to express the joy I experienced as I opened the door and went from room to room. The furniture consisted of a home-made mattress covered with sacking, four and a half feet long, four benches, one rough board sofa, five tables and one chair. My heart leaped for joy ; this was more than I had expected. After shovelling snow for an hour and a half I put up my stove, and then with what boards I could find, I fixed an addition to my bed of a foot and a half that it might be long enough to hold me. The last missionary must have been an unusually short man. That night I called a meeting of the chief Indians and arranged the details of the work.

I believe I suffered more during the week that followed than ever before. Night after night I shivered in my cold, scanty bed. During the day I was kept busy trying to get the wet wood to burn, but instead I filled the house with smoke and got but little heat. Often I came home dripping wet from head to foot, to a house that was bitter cold, and had to build a fire, change my clothes and wait for sufficient heat to dry me. Sometimes my feet were so wet and cold that they felt like lumps of ice, nor could I get warm at all until the stove was hot.

But so great was the joy of the Lord in my soul that I sometimes ran up and down the room until almost out of breath, singing, "Praise God from Whom All Blessings Flow", in spite of my wet condition and my ice-cold feet, before taking time to light the fire. Thus I entered into some of the experiences of missionary life. My greatest difficulty was my fire. At first I got a few sticks from the saw-mill, and tried to start it, but after lighting it nearly a score of times, I finally gave up. Then I tore a board off the back shed, cut it up and tried again. This time it burned, but did not heat the room.

Never will I forget that first night. Oh, how lonely it was ! I was the only white person on the reserve. I shivered in my bed. As I lay there it dawned upon me with terrific force that I was alone among the Indians. For a long time I lay awake. Every sound startled me, and I listened, almost afraid to move. At last I fell asleep, but awakened several times during the night. I was now nineteen.

Four times each week I preached to the Indians. They nearly

all attended. God was with us and abundantly blessed, making our hearts to glow with joy. During the week I taught school, having the unique experience of teaching Indian children.

The Indians, contrary to their agreement, failed to supply me with wood, and I suffered much from the severe cold. Finally I borrowed a dug-out, took a bright Indian boy with me, an axe, and a cross-cut saw, and rowed across the bay. He soon spotted a yellow cedar, near the water's edge—the only wood that would burn green. Cutting it down, we slid it into the water and started back, but what with the labour of getting it afloat, the high swells, the difficulty of towing it, it was half a day before I had it sawn up and split for the stove.

Deer abounded everywhere. At one time an Indian was only out for an hour and returned with ten. Thus I was kept in fresh venison. Then too, I had all the skins I wanted for mats. Hundreds of wild ducks fed daily within a stone's throw.

At last the cold weather began breaking up. The river thawed and the snow melted. With the exception of three families, the Indians all left for the hunting grounds. Night after night I was awakened by a terrific noise, the roar of the snow, piled four feet high, as it crashed off the roof. One morning, upon going out, I found my back shed lying under four feet of snow, the entire roof having given away. What if it had fallen when I was in it!

One evening when I was out in my dug-out with the Chinese cook from the saw-mill across the river, he rowing, I gazing into the depths of the sea, suddenly the oarlock came out, and Chung tumbled on my feet. Immediately the canoe sank and the water poured in right over my legs and poor Chung's back. He was terribly frightened, for he couldn't swim a stroke, and we were half a mile out. In a moment I saw that the other end of the canoe was out of water, and quicker than I can write, I told him to jump to the bow, at the same time pointing and giving him a push. He was just in time. The dug-out came up as I was preparing to leap out, about two-thirds full of water. We bailed it out and soon reached land, but it was a close shave. Thus God preserved.

As the days grew warmer and the weather more beautiful, I spent many a happy hour in my dug-out on the sparkling waters of the ocean, and enjoyed to the full guiding my frail bark through the rough cross currents, or among the rocks where the breakers roared and broke in white foam as I landed. One never-to-be-forgotten day still lingers in my memory, the day I rowed my canoe to a rocky ledge in order to escape from a giant eagle that seemed intent on attacking me.

THE VOICE OF GOD

About this time, while alone in the mission house, I was led out in definite prayer regarding my future. And may I say that I can never forget the sweet fellowship and communion with Christ that was mine during the days I lived alone among the Indians. Night after night I prayed, kneeling before a chair in the dim light of a coal oil lamp, all around me the mighty forest, dark and wild, in my ears the roar of the ocean, and on every side the homes of the Indians. My little stove burned but poorly as I shoved in green cedar. At times my thoughts were far away. I sat and dreamed of home. Oh for a glimpse of the dear ones again! My mother—I could see her in imagination. Was she thinking of me? Had she ever dreamed that her nineteen-year-old son, her first born, would one day be living among the Indians? How my heart beat as my eyes filled with tears!

It was too much. Unable to bear more, I quietly slid to my knees and turned my face upward to God. I was not alone. He knew. He was with me. Oh, what a Friend! And as I prayed, there came the oft-repeated request: "Lord, what wilt Thou have me to do?"

How long I prayed I do not know. But at last I undressed, replenished the fire, put out the light and crawled into my poor, hand-made bed. Suddenly God spoke. The answer came. "Go to the Toronto Bible Training School," said the Voice. I heard no sound, and yet the command was so clearly given that I could not mistake it.

At last, on April 29th, my labours at Hartley Bay came to an end, and I returned to colportage work for the Bible Society. Often I preached in churches and mission halls as well as on the street.

From April 29th to September 24th, I travelled by train and boat all up and down the lower coast, selling Bibles. How many times God delivered me it would be impossible to say. Time after time I had occasion to thank Him for the text given me by Hetty Humphrey, a fellow student at the Toronto Bible

B

College: "My God shall supply all your need according to His riches in glory by Christ Jesus" (Phil. 4: 19). Again and again I proved it. Sometimes I did not know where my next meal was coming from. Often I owed a week's board. Frequently I was unable to pay my fare. But in each instance I pled the promise and God always answered. A Bible was sold just in the nick of time, and I went on my way rejoicing.

Often I look back and wonder how I ever did it. I think of my two sons, Glen and Paul, when they were nineteen, and to imagine them in a similar position makes me shiver. Certainly I was far too young to be roughing it among Indians and construction men more than three thousand miles from home. Sin abounded on every side. I was in constant danger. But God watched over me and brought me safely through. Blessed be His Name!

CHAPTER III

ACROSS THE PRAIRIES

I NOW had to reach a decision as to my future course. The Methodist Superintendent of Missions, Dr. White, offered me a church at Greenwood, with the understanding that I would prepare myself for the Methodist ministry. At the same time Dr. Baird of Manitoba College, Winnipeg, answered a letter I had sent him stating that I could take the Minister-Evangelist course there and thus enter the ministry of the Presbyterian Church. For a while I was undecided. Finally I chose Winnipeg, and on September 24th, 1909, I left Vancouver for the East, after having spent a full year in British Columbia. The mountains were now left behind, and the prairies opened before me.

No words of mine can ever express the bitter disappointment and terrible agony of soul when I was told that I could not take the special five-year course, but that I must settle down to the regular nine years' work. I had come all the way from Vancouver to Winnipeg to enter Manitoba College to study for the ministry. But—I had disobeyed God, for I should have gone to the Toronto Bible Training School. Oh, how I struggled, and wept and prayed! Only God knows. At last I entered the classes of the regular course and commenced my freshman's year.

It was at Manitoba College that I had my first and only experience of initiation. Space forbids a detailed account. Suffice it to say that we were dragged out of our rooms at twelve o'clock one night, three times "bounced" in a large blanket some thirty feet high, then tied to a beam in the basement with a large, dirty rope, after that covered with thick red paint, and then nearly drowned with the cold water hose. Finally we were herded into a room and compelled to sing, play or recite for the benefit of the sophomores.

On hallowe'en night we had a wild time, as students usually do. About one hundred and fifty of us put on our nightshirts

35

and paraded the main streets of Winnipeg, creating quite a sensation. The homes of the various professors were visited, including Ralph Connor's, where a barrel of apples awaited us. We gave our yell and raided three theatres and a street car, pulling the pole off the trolley, "bounced" pedestrians who voiced their objections, and ended up by storming Wesley Methodist College, where we fought our way upstairs in the face of a fearful barrage of water from a large hose, found the fellow who had turned it on us, almost drowned him, tore the hose away, and bore it triumphantly back to our own College.

Dr. Riddell, Canada's Commissioner to the League of Nations, Geneva, and the Hon. James Gardiner, Canada's Minister of Agriculture, Ottawa, were my fellow students. Also the Right Rev. John McNab, D.D., later Moderator.

December 25th, 1909, was a happy day for me, a happiness completely expressed in one word—home. Yes, I went home after an absence of a year and four months, and, incidentally, attended the great Rochester Convention of Student Volunteers where I was tremendously moved by Dr. John R. Mott, Robert E. Speer and Sherwood Eddy.

But oh, what a joy it was to see the dear home faces once more! My mother came through the snow to meet me at the Mount Albert station, and as we walked back she kept her arms tightly around me and wept most of the way. Father walked by my side. What a thrill it gave me to feel their love! That was a real home-coming. How I thanked the Lord again and again for permitting me to see them once more! The last Christmas I had spent among the Indians, this one, at home. When I left I was a boy of eighteen; now I had turned twenty.

Rev. D. G. Cameron, the Presbyterian minister at Mount Albert, very kindly permitted me to take a service in his church, and so for the first time my parents heard me preach.

Upon my return to Manitoba College I was taken quite ill with rheumatism and had to spend some time in the public ward of the hospital. Later I had the joy of seeing Miss Hetty Humphrey on her way to Fort Simpson. She is now with Christ.

It would be impossible for me to relate all the thrilling experiences through which I passed, my trips over the prairie through awful storms of wind and snow, the times I barely escaped death from some four or five bad runaways that I had, the terrible blizzards that sometimes compelled me to turn back, the lonely prairie homes that I visited, the joys and blessings as well as the hardships of preaching the Gospel in a land where it is so easy to miss the way and be left to the elements.

On March 5th, 1910, I wrote in my diary as follows: "I long to get nearer to God. Oh that all sin might be overcome and that I might be filled with the Spirit! I do so want to win souls. How I yearn for evangelistic work! May God lead me into it!"

Again from my diary: "April 24th, 1910—I cannot doubt but that God has a great work for me, and that in the future years I will preach the Gospel to thousands.

"May 10th, 1910—My one great thought day and night is evangelism! Even while studying my thoughts run off and I see myself preaching to crowds of people in an evangelistic meeting. Sometimes I can scarcely stand it. Oh, how often I have walked the floor, planning, praying and wondering when the time would come. I lie awake at night thinking and dreaming of it. Oh, how I long to be wholly surrendered to God that He may use me! May the time soon come when He will enable me to rescue hundreds of lost souls.

"May 16th, 1910: Have just had a wonderful open-air meeting on the streets of Winnipeg. God gave us great freedom; and although the night was cold, still, many stood around and listened. Oh, may some poor dying soul receive our precious Saviour!

"May 24th, 1910: May God enable me to do a lasting work for Him before many more years have fled! The great burden regarding my life's work came upon me again as I knelt in prayer Sunday night! The question of whether or not to spend another year in College seemed to be suddenly decided. While praying, a calm, clear assurance came over me that I would not return. God has laid upon my heart the great responsibility of winning souls, and my heart is aflame with zeal to make soul-winning my life's work."

HOLLYWOOD

I left Winnipeg on June 2nd, 1910, and spent the summer on the Mission Field, living at Hollywood, Manitoba, which I reached by a thirty-mile stage ride through a wilderness of brush and small trees.

After making some pastoral calls in the settlement one day,

I started home with a new horse. I had the whip in my hand and was just putting it in its place when it touched the horse. He sprang away at once, right in the brush, over logs and stumps. It was all I could do to hang on. Then he began to kick as he ran, until the cart bounded hither and thither in a fearful manner. Climbing over the back, I attempted to hang on, but was nearly thrown in the wheel several times. Suddenly the cart struck a large stump and I was thrown off: I struck on my hips, and although badly skinned and bruised, thank God, no bones were broken. The cart turned upside down, the horse tore away, and I trudged the three miles home on foot.

That night I had a dream, very clear and realistic. I was in the stall sleeping with the horse. The horse began to move and I decided to take the next stall. I was very cold, and, remembering a blanket that hung near the stall, I attempted to pull it down. Harder and harder I pulled, but it would not come. I awoke and found myself out of bed, standing up and tugging at a sheet that served as a partition between my hostess, Mrs. Morehead, her daughters, and myself.

I found the people careless but hungry. No minister had visited some of them for years. My heart was wrung with anguish again and again as I realized that they were forced to live their lonely lives with so few opportunities of hearing the Gospel. There was much bad feeling among the people, and all I needed to discourage me. Three times my horse ran away and came near killing me. But now to quote again from my diary:

"June 20th, 1910: Before I came to this field I was led to pray for the conversion of souls. Since coming God has laid the burden of a revival upon me, and oh, how I long to see souls saved! I have been reading the 'Autobiography of Chas. G. Finney', and God has used it to awaken me. I have discovered that I must lay the very greatest stress on prayer and the work of the Holy Spirit to convert men. But oh, how weak and feeble I am!

"I went to hold my first service some thirteen miles north last night. The devil very nearly discouraged me. The day was fearfully hot, and as I drove beneath a scorching sun, myriads of mosquitos bit me all over, while the terrible 'bull-dogs' (large flies), stung my horse until it was almost wild. My head throbbed and ached, and I was ready to give up, but God sustained, and we had a good meeting.

"June 22nd, 1910: This morning I spent over two hours in prayer in the wood. Dealt with my own need and prayed for revival.

"June 23rd: God has been pressing upon me the necessity of a Spirit-filled life ever since I started to read Chas. G. Finney. While driving home I prayed for Him to strip me of anything that hindered. He had searched my heart. Most of this morning I have spent in communion with Him. As far as I know I surrendered all. Then placing my finger on Luke 11:13, 'If ye then, being evil, know how to give good gifts unto your children: how much more shall your heavenly Father give the Holy Spirit to them that ask him?' I claimed the promise, and I believe He has filled me. Praise God! The manifestation that came to Finney did not come to me, nor does the Bible promise it; but I believe the manifestation will be seen in the effect on souls as I bear witness for Him.

"June 30th: My life in some way or other is changed. My mind is at rest. Even in the midst of physical suffering there is real heart peace. Yet I wait for the great and glorious manifestation of seeing souls won for Christ.

"Spent all Monday in the saddle visiting the people, but it being my first day on horse-back, I became very weary and tired. Returning home I lost the trail, so rode directly through the bush and struck it again on the other side. After proceeding for some distance I came to a wire fence. It was quite dark, so I dismounted and led my horse, seeking an opening. After searching in vain I stopped and called upon God for guidance. Immediately I was impressed to return. So, facing about, I retraced my steps all the way back, but was suddenly halted by another fence. Then I knew not what to do, and had just concluded to abandon my horse for the night, when God directed my eye to a post, which, upon examination, I discovered to be a gateway. Filled with praise for another answer to prayer, I remounted and arrived home an hour before midnight."

Some of my experiences were of a most discouraging nature. I held services on Sunday at which there were only two present. I held prayer meetings when only one came out. Many of the people lived far back in the bush and were very poor. Some only had one room for everything. I remember one place where they put me to sleep up in a loft, and as I was afraid I might get up in my sleep and step off the edge of the outside board, fall to the room below and thus break a leg or worse, I tied one end of a rope around my wrist and the other end to the bed, and thus went to sleep. One day a woman said to me, "We will hear you in the Old Country yet," a prediction that came true.

GOD'S CARE

Every now and again something or other of a rather exciting nature was mine. In the darkness one night, while driving through a field, I drove over a large hole and barely missed plunging in, horse and all. Thomas M. Thomas, my Armenian friend from Winnipeg, spent his holidays with me. We had many adventures together shooting ducks and prairie chickens. One experience that might have become a tragedy I can never forget.

I was crawling through the tall grass, pulling myself along inch by inch on my stomach toward the duck pond, in order not to be seen or heard. A young boy was crawling just ahead of me. My double-barrel shotgun kept passing back and forth behind him as he crept along. Suddenly the trigger caught on something and the gun went off. It had just swung past his body and the shot tore by within an inch or two of his hip. Had it fired a second sooner it would have killed him on the spot. How I thanked God for His providential care! It was the nearest I have ever come to taking human life.

I had rather a unique experience of God's care and answer to prayer on my way home from the Presbytery meeting at Portage la Prairie. My ticket was purchased to a station within 18 miles of Hollywood, since the train only ran to Hollywood on Monday nights. I expected to have to walk the remainder of the way home. In the station I became desperately sick and could scarcely stand. I felt very faint. The train was late, but at last it arrived and I held out as well as I could until I reached the station where I was to get off, eighteen miles from home. I found, however, that I could hardly stand, and so sat down to think things over.

I had just made up my mind to start out and try to walk to a farmer's home about four miles away where I thought I might be able to stay for the night, when I was suddenly informed by one of the trainmen that they were going right through to Hollywood that night. I got back on and in a short time arrived home. This was the only time during the entire summer that the train had come to Hollywood on any other night but Monday. I had asked God to either provide a way for me to get home or to give me strength to walk the eighteen miles. How wonderfully He worked! Even trains can be placed at the disposal of God's children, in answer to prayer, when He so wills it.

I spent a good deal of time waiting upon God regarding the next step. It would be impossible for me to tell of the blessing received through the reading of biography. I studied the lives of some of God's choicest saints, both missionaries and evangelists, and received wonderful inspiration and help. God made me willing to do His will, whether at home or in the foreign field. After praying much I felt definitely led to go back to Toronto, there to attend the Bible College, and so fit myself for His service. I had no desire to continue my course in Manitoba College, Winnipeg, although I still wanted to be a Presbyterian minister. As a matter of fact, I applied to Knox College, Toronto, but was rejected because of insufficient education.

At last the time came to leave. On Sunday, October 2nd, 1910, I preached my farewell sermon, then taking the train as far as Lake Superior, I boarded the *Athabasca,* one of the lake vessels, crossed to the other side, and finally arrived in Toronto.

Having missed my connections, I was compelled to spend Sunday in Toronto, and I went to St. Mark's Presbyterian Church, where my friend, Rev. J. D. Morrow, was still pastor. The services were being held in St. Andrew's Hall, since the old church had been sold and the new one, Dale, had not yet been finished. Mr. Morrow saw me coming up the aisle and smiled his welcome. He took me home to dinner and had me address his Bible Class in the afternoon.

Next morning I caught my train for Mount Albert, and in due time reached my destination. What a joy it was to be home once again!

CHAPTER IV

STUDENT YEARS

MY THEOLOGICAL studies, strictly speaking, cover a period of five years, two years in the Toronto Bible College and three in McCormick Theological Seminary, Chicago; 1910 to 1915, or from the time I was twenty until I was twenty-five years of age. Later I took special work in Knox College, Toronto. Previously, of course, I had attended the evening classes in the Bible College, and had taken the one year in Manitoba College.

Upon my return to Toronto, I immediately began to attend the lectures in the Bible College each morning. And oh, how happy I was to enter that hall of sacred memories once again, and to listen, as before, to the exposition of God's Word by the Principal, Rev. John McNicol, D.D.; Rev. Elmore Harris, D.D., the Founder and President, Rev. Wm. Stewart, D.D.; Rev. Andrew Imrie, Rev. T. Bradley Hyde, Dr. J. Griffith-Thomas, and others.

At the same time I took up dentistry on the side, working in the office of Dr. Adams, in the Jewish ward, where I learned a little about filling and extracting teeth in pre-preparation for work in the foreign field, should God so lead. During the winter months I taught a class in the Central Prison at nine o'clock each Sunday morning.

It was while attending the Bible College that I became really interested in Missions, and surrendered my life to God for foreign service. "Unless God prevents," I wrote, "I will go to the Foreign Field."

One day I had the audacity to telephone Rev. A. W. Roffe, pastor of the Missionary Tabernacle on Bathurst St., to ask him if I might hold a two weeks' campaign. Impossible as it may seem, for I was a stranger to him, he agreed. This was my first evangelistic campaign. I got out 3,000 hand-bills and had them distributed by 17 boys from Wesley Hunnisett's class in

Wesley Methodist Church, boys who had accepted Christ in
one of my meetings. Miss Jennie M. Tyrrell, of the Nursing At
Home Mission, a deeply spiritual worker from St. George, and
a former graduate (1909) of the Bible College, sang for me,
and Rev. J. D. Morrow came and helped. I preached each
night and a few professed conversion. That was in January,
1911, when I was twenty-one.

The great Chapman-Alexander Simultaneous Evangelistic
Campaign was held in Toronto that winter, and I ushered
and did personal work in Massey Hall. Again Robert Harkness was the pianist. Miss Tyrrell was often with me in these
meetings. Many souls were won and my young heart was
filled with joy. One night I found myself sitting beside and
talking to Rev. H. T. Crossley, the noted Methodist evangelist.

Through the winter I helped at the free breakfast hour in
Yonge Street Mission, and, when occasion offered, preached
or did personal work there as well as in the King's Mission, the
Sackville Mission, and other centres.

When the Spring came I applied to the Presbyterian Church
for evangelistic work for the summer, but in a letter from the
chairman of the Board, Rev. F. A. Robinson, I was refused. I
then became Canada's first Travelling Secretary for the Pocket
Testament League, and had the privilege of presenting the
work in the various churches of Galt, Preston, Waterloo,
Guelph, Kitchener and Woodstock. A letter which I received
from Fanny J. Crosby, the blind hymn writer, that year was a
great help to me in connection with the work of the League.

Toward the close of the summer I visited Embro, my old
home, once more. It was the first time I had seen it since we
had left five years before. I walked to the old station where I
had lived as a boy, wandered around the school grounds at
Cody's Corners, and took a number of pictures. Once again I
talked to old Mrs. Sutherland, who had been so kind to us
when we were boys. My former school chums, Arthur Waring,
Florence Sharpe, Andrew Cody and others gave me a hearty
welcome. Dr. Green, our physician, took me to see the grave
of my sister Hazel. Oh, what memories! That was in 1911.

It was during my first year in the Toronto Bible College that
I entered into one of the sweetest, one of the most sacred experiences of my life. Soon after I returned for my second
year, viz., on October 19th, 1911, I became engaged to the
lovely Christian nurse whom I had met in the Nursing At

Home Mission on November 22nd, 1910, and who often sang for me in my meetings. It was a romance that ennobled my entire life, changed my whole outlook, and drew me closer to God than ever before. Her letters were filled with Christ, holiness, love and missions. She knew no guile. It was a sacred and holy relationship.

About this time I became pastor of the Congregational Church at Belwood, Ont., and I ministered each Sunday at Belwood and Garafrasi throughout the winter and summer of 1911-12. I received about $7.00 a week, clear. Thus God provided for all my needs. Dr. McNicol had chosen me for this work.

I came very near leaving the Bible College one day, shortly before graduation, when I was publicly reprimanded by Rev. Andrew Imrie for unintentionally disturbing the class. But through the influence of my fiancée, God overruled and I stayed.

On April 26th, 1912, I graduated from the Toronto Bible College and had the honour of delivering the Valedictory address.

Never can I thank God enough for these two years. My whole life was utterly changed. As a result of the study of God's Word I was forever safe-guarded against Higher Criticism. I was appointed leader of the Evangelistic Band and thus gained a great deal of practical experience in conducting meetings. Fred Vine, Maude Sweetman, Fred Story, Glen Wardell, Harry Bowers, Percy Near, Edna Fallis, and others, took part in the services which we held. And Jennie M. Tyrrell very frequently went with us to sing.

"Dwell Deep" was our motto. Our prayer meetings were times of refreshing. As we sat taking lectures we felt as though we were in Heaven itself, so wonderful was the atmosphere, for we were brought face to face with God. Our trials and sorrows, our joys and triumphs, were mutually shared, for we were all one family in Christ. We grew to know Him better. And the knowledge of the Scriptures imparted by our godly instructors, has been of untold value to us throughout the years.

During my summer at Belwood I brought some thirty-five children from the slums of Toronto, and had the joy of placing them on farms in the country for a vacation.

My ministry at Belwood and Garafrasi came to a close about the first of September. I had had full charge of all the services, and had preached both morning and evening on Sundays, for about a year. There was a splendid attendance and I received the very training that I needed. Bella Townsend was our organist.

MCCORMICK THEOLOGICAL SEMINARY

After much prayer I decided to continue my studies for the ministry in McCormick Theological Seminary, Chigago. I felt that I owed it to my future wife to secure my full standing as a Presbyterian minister. And so, after visiting my family and friends and preaching my farewell message in Dale Presbyterian Church, with the Rev. J. D. Morrow on the platform, and some of my dear ones, including my mother and fiancée, in the audience, I left for Chicago on September 9th, 1912. Jennie travelled with me as far as Brantford, where we parted. Only God knows how hard it was to leave the one I so dearly loved, but never did it dawn on me to even think of marriage during my student days.

Chicago made a deep impression on me. Its enormous population, its great distances, its magnificent parks and boulevards, perhaps the finest in the world, could not help but arrest my attention. But most of all the many centres of evangelism, especially the world-famous Moody Church. Little did I think then, as I attended the services, eagerly drinking in the evangelistic fervor created by the large choir under the leadership of Dr. D. B. Towner, that I would one day preach from that famous pulpit.

But then, too, there was the other side—segregated, legalized vice, and all the wickedness and sin of a great metropolis. Many a time I was oppressed in spirit, until I yearned as never before for the return of the Lord Jesus Christ. However, I grew to love Chicago and to look upon it as my second home.

On November 8th, 1912, I wrote in my diary, in part, as follows: "My twenty-third birthday. I thank God for twenty-three years of life. I praise Him for the way He has led me and for all His goodness to me these twenty-three years. I am glad He called me to Himself, and I pray that He may spare me to serve Him for another twenty-three years.

"This morning I re-consecrated my life to Him. I long to be more faithful. I have been very discontented and impatient, but God has used my dearest one to bring me into a place of humility before Him. As we look upon sin we become like it; as we gaze upon Christ, we become like Him."

Another entry. "November 20th, 1912: I have been reading the diary of David Brainerd. He died to self. May I too die and live only for God's glory. How proud I am! How independent! May He deliver me from the sin of ambition, the vain glory of life. Brainerd has put a deeper longing in my heart for the foreign field. He has taught me to pray.

"November 30th, 1912: At the Moody Church. Pictures of India. It is now my definite aim to give my life for the non-Christian world. The opportunities at home seem small indeed in comparison to the privilege of giving the Gospel to those who have never heard. It is only in His will that I can be happy. Gladly do I offer myself for the Mission Field. What is the world's popularity in comparison to God's 'Well done!' My heart was deeply touched as I listened to the appeal. Surely I can do something to help. The presence of Jesus is very real to me tonight.

"December 9th, 1912: I am afraid I am getting into financial difficulties, for I only have ninety-five cents left. I am taking but two meals a day in order to save money. I have been doing this for the past two years. However, I have laid the whole matter before God, pleading Phil. 4: 19, and I know that He will somehow bring me through. Have been giving a little to Missions, besides trying to meet my Seminary expenses. This afternoon I endeavoured to secure work as a waiter in a restaurant, but failed. However, I am not worried for I know God will answer.

"I have taken charge of a Boys' Club in the Bohemian Settlement House, a wild, rough gang. Only God can tame them.

"My soul is filled with love to Christ today. I was fearfully tested, but I lifted my heart in prayer to God, and cried for deliverance. He heard. Oh, how precious! Blessed, blessed Saviour! My eyes were wet with tears as I experienced anew His wonderful love.

"December 13th, 1912: I have joined Buena Memorial Presbyterian Church, of which the Rev. Henry Hepburn, D.D., is the pastor. He has been a great friend and has encouraged me many a time.

"February 19th, 1913: About two weeks ago I was sent by Rev. George L. Robinson, D.D., one of my professors, to supply the pulpit of the Millard Avenue Presbyterian Church

in South-west Chicago. And now I have been called as Acting
Pastor at a salary of ten dollars a week. Hallelujah! God has
answered. All my needs are abundantly supplied. Phil. 4 : 19
still holds good."

On May 4th, 1913, I closed my ministry in Millard Avenue,
(now Lawndale) Presbyterian Church. While I was there God
gave me twelve precious souls. They were so broken in spirit
that they wept their way through to Calvary. Mrs. Reid and
her two daughters entertained me.

AMONG THE MOUNTAINEERS

On May 6th I left for my summer's work in Kentucky. I
had been reading the novels of John Fox, and as a result I
decided to preach the Gospel to the mountaineers of Kentucky.
From Harlan, where I got off the train, I had to ride horseback
to Cawood through the Cumberland mountains, occasionally
fording a swift running stream. The scenery was magnificent.
Laurel and rhododendron covered the hills. Birds sang in the
trees. Log cabins nestled in the valleys, and game abounded
on every side.

Here feuds have been fought for generations. Hot corn
bread is the staff of life. Plenty of fat pork, squirrel, chicken,
rabbit and fish, all cooked in grease, is the menu. The potatoes
are seldom boiled. They are sometimes baked, but generally
fried in grease. Tea is practically unknown. Their drink is
coffee or milk, preferably sour milk.

At Cawood there is a church, a school and a manse. I lived
alone in the manse, got my own breakfast, and ate my other
meals in the humble home of a Mrs. Noe. Mr. Carter was the
Sunday School Superintendent. I rode muleback over the
mountains and through the valleys to my various preaching
appointments. It was all very enjoyable, yet oh, so lonely!

MY GREAT SORROW

Over the tragic experience of April, 1913, when I was only
23 years of age, I must for the present draw a veil. Only God
knows the sorrow and heartache, the bitter, bitter disappointment, the days of suffering and suspense. Some of my best
known hymns and poems were born out of those hours of
anguish and grief.

"My heart is shattered and broken," I wrote in my diary, "but God is my portion. Sorrow has made Christ very real; communion with Him is the sweetest thing on earth. Oh, how near He seems!

"This has been a day of consecration and surrender," I continued writing on May 17th. "As far as I know I have yielded all. I have been reading Whittier and have been impressed with these words: *'I only ask a will resigned, O Father, to Thine own'*."

Then—and let me say it to the glory of God—on May 22nd, suddenly, unexpectedly, the impossible happened. *My heart was instantly healed,* yes, healed, and that in spite of my great loss. My dreams had perished but His grace triumphed. And even now I can recall the glow of holy fervour and joy with which I commemorated that miraculous experience by writing the poem, "Sorrow's Benediction."

Weeks before, when I was driven to distraction by anxiety and suspense, God, one day, gave me Psalm 30: 5, "Weeping may endure for a night, but joy cometh in the morning," and that night I slept in perfect peace. For a long time the "weeping" continued, but I believed God, and on May 22nd, 1913, among the mountains of Kentucky, the "morning" dawned and the "joy" came. True, I did not forget. The wounds healed, but the scars remained.

"May 23rd, 1913: Wonderfully reconciled. God is answering prayer and making me submissive to His will. The trial has been hard to bear, but the light is beginning to break. Wonderful, wonderful peace! Human love has failed, but my heart cries out, 'O Love that will not let me go!'

"May 31st, 1913: I had a marvellous season of communion with God this morning. Was greatly blessed in reading Romans 6: 14, 'Sin shall not have dominion over you'. Oh, the joy of fellowship with God! No other love is so sweet as His love. How I long to be used. I feel that He has a great work for me somewhere, but where I do not know. My prayer is 'Lord, make me submissive'.

"June 3rd, 1913: Sick and discouraged. My life seems so useless, so worthless. My dreams of service have never yet come true. Will I ever find God's place for me? I am doing so little, oh, so little.

"June 4th, 1913: I have made a new surrender to God and have dealt with every known sin in my life. Have been reading 'Tauler' by Whittier. Was gripped by this thought: *'And for the happiness of which I spake, I find it in submission to His will.'* This, and the statement: 'If I regard iniquity in my heart, the Lord will not hear me' (Psalm 66: 18), drove me to God. I prayed and prayed, confessing and surrendering, and a wonderful joy and peace entered my torn and bleeding heart, so that I was enabled to resign myself to the will of God. I never dreamed that such joy could be mine. But, praise God, it is. And He is now my portion, for He has satisfied me with Himself. Glory to His Name!

"June 9th, 1913: I will never be able to tell what a blessing 'The Threefold Secret of the Holy Spirit', by Jas. H. McConkey, has been to me. I have read it twice. Oh, how I long to know the secret of power for service! I am now twenty-three years of age. I have preached over four hundred sermons, but oh, how much there has been of self. Thank God, my heartache has driven me to Him. I am now laying this torn, broken, defeated, selfish, conceited, proud, ambitious life at His feet.

"June 13th, 1913: This morning I had the joy of spending an hour and a quarter in prayer. God was very near. Oh, the peace the Saviour gives! Truly, it 'passeth understanding'. More and more He enables me to yield my will, my plans and my dreams to Him.

"July 27th, 1913: I am sitting all alone on my verandah. Overhead the clouds hang motionless. Away in the west the setting sun is tinting the sleeping hills, and they are beautiful beyond description. It reminds me of the gate of Heaven. All is still. And I am happy, oh, so happy, for the peace of the Eternal God floods my soul. I am here for Him, here to lead these poor, humble mountain people to a knowledge of life in Christ. And the very stillness itself speaks to me of God. Yet I long for activity. The Call of the great, throbbing city is ever with me. Almost daily I think of evangelistic work. Voices loud and insistent speak within my soul.

A NARROW ESCAPE

"July 29th, 1913: Have just had a most exciting experience, but thanks be to God, I am alive to tell the tale. It happened on this wise:

"There is a district here that has long been known as the

worst community in the County. It is the centre of a number of 'moonshine stills' where whisky is made contrary to law. Mr. Burkhart, a fine Christian mountaineer, and I, determined to hold a series of evangelistic meetings in this place, for we felt that the need was great. The schoolhouse was well filled every night, but with the exception of two or three women who accepted Christ, absolutely no interest whatever was shown. The meetings were no sooner concluded than scores of shots were heard in different directions. On one occasion a bullet passed between a mule's legs upon which a woman was riding. Another shattered a lantern in a man's hand. And still a third buried itself in a house, just missing the owner, who was sitting on the verandah.

"When Friday night came we announced that there would be another meeting on Monday at 4 p.m. That night we both returned home for our regular Sunday work. Monday came and I was just preparing to saddle my mule when I was surprised to receive a visit from Charley Pope, a young mountaineer, who told me that a gang of low-down men, led by two of the worst characters in the community, were to blacken their faces that they might not be recognized, hide somewhere in the mountain I had to cross, spring out upon me as I came along alone, and beat me up.

"Their plans were carefully laid. The plot seemed to promise well. But somehow or other one of their women found it out, and to her, under God, I owe my escape, perhaps from death. Leaving her home late at night, she made her way with all possible speed to warn me, and reached my friend's house in the early morning. Here she told her story, making him promise not to reveal her identity. She wept much while unfolding the plot, for some of her own relatives were connected with it. Charley carried it the rest of the way, and told me just before I had saddled the mule, strongly advising me not to go.

"For a few moments I thought it over, but finally concluded that it was my duty to keep my appointment and preach the Gospel. Finding Mr. Carter, I told him of the plot and asked him to accompany me. Together we rode over the mountain. Soon after crossing, we observed the two leaders coming down after us. We held the meeting at the appointed hour and prepared to return before dark. We were now three strong, Charley having joined us. Leaving the leaders of the gang scowling at us, their wicked-looking faces betraying keen disappointment, we started up the mountain again, and soon after reached the other side, safe and sound.

"I could never describe how I felt when I realized my escape. My heart was too full for words as I returned thanks to God, who had delivered me out of the snare of violent men, and had caused that brave mountain woman to come so far to warn me of my danger. Next morning my reading lesson happened to be the twenty-second chapter of Second Samuel, and I could not help but marvel at the strange coincidence.

THE TURTLE CREEK REVIVAL

"August 10th, 1913: Discouraged. No results. People indifferent. I am so tired and weak. I walked four and a half miles to visit a sick man and then rode a mule six miles in the boiling sun. Fearful headache. I have one so often now and they last for hours. Lay on my bed and cried for relief. Toward evening, walked three miles and preached. No strength, but, praise God, three souls were saved.

"August 20th, 1913: We have just had a revival in a place called Turtle Creek. But it started, I am convinced, on a hot, disagreeable Sunday morning, some two months ago. My sermon had been delivered with much labour and difficulty. Spirit, enthusiasm, energy and freedom were lacking. Even the atmosphere seemed oppressive. But I had decided that morning that I would give the people a chance to accept Christ. Almost immediately, four indicated by the uplifted hand their desire to be saved.

"Over two weeks ago Mr. Burkhart and I started a series of evangelistic meetings at this needy place, preaching the Gospel every night, visiting in the homes, praying with the people, and doing personal work through the day. Almost immediately God began to work. The building was filled, many of the men having to stand around the walls. Night after night they came forward, until, at last, no less than forty-one had accepted Christ. Immediately they began to testify and to lead others to the Saviour.

"At our closing meeting we had the Rev. Carl T. Michel, pastor of the Presbyterian Church at Harlan, with us, who delivered the message and sang with deep pathos and feeling some of the old gospel songs. It seemed like the pleading voice of the Saviour Himself, as the message to the new converts was given in the words of that immortal hymn, 'Throw Out the Life Line'. Few of those who were present will ever forget the yearning tones of pity and love with which Mr. Michael sang the closing words of the chorus, 'Someone is sinking today'.

"As for me, God has shown me He can and will use me. And now, more than ever, I feel the call to evangelistic work, a call that has throbbed in my heart for seven long years. But, regardless of what the future may bring, I am determined that God shall have all there is of Oswald J. Smith.

"August 28th, 1913: Thrown from a horse and badly bruised. Had another runaway, this time a mule. God alone preserved me. Wrote my poem, 'The Voices'.

"September 1st, 1913: Twice already I have lived alone, first, when I was nineteen, among the Indians, and now, at twenty-three, with the mountaineers. Never can I forget the lonely evenings at Hartley Bay. Nor will I ever forget the long, oppressive afternoons here at Cawood, where the sun fairly scorches, or the lonely evenings when the night is dark, and the house still. How often I have thought of home! Truly, it is not good for a man to live alone. He needs companionship.

"September 8th, 1913. Twelve have professed conversion. He condescends to use me, unworthy though I am. This summer I have seen 63 decisions for Christ.

"September 17th, 1913: It is night, my last night at Cawood. My summer's work is ended, and tomorrow I start for Chicago again. A mule will carry me to Harlan. As I sit alone in my little cottage, I feel more contented and happier than ever before. Truly, God has given me the promised joy He spoke to me about last April; and He has taken away the grief and the sorrow. Oh, how wonderful! I never dreamed it would be possible for me to be happy again. I came to Cawood weak and broken-hearted, in the midst of the greatest sorrow of my life. I leave it well and happy, but, above all, hopeful again, for I view the future with the greatest optimism.

BACK IN CHICAGO

"September 22nd, 1913: Back in Chicago. I feel fine and am ready for a good winter's work. The peace of God continues to abide within my heart and I am in high spirits. I don't know when I have been happier. Truly, 'Weeping may endure for a night, but joy cometh in the morning'. Hallelujah!

"October 5th, 1913: Tonight, on my knees, I wrote out and signed this three-fold dedication of myself to God:

1. *I will think no thought, speak no word, and do no deed unworthy of a follower of Jesus Christ.*
2. *I will give my life for service in any part of the world, and in any capacity God wills that I should labour.*
3. *I shall endeavour to do God's will from moment to moment, as He reveals it to me.*

"October 21st, 1913: A direct answer to prayer. Today I became pastor of the South Chicago Presbyterian Church at a salary of $60.00 a month.

"October 25th, 1913: Finished reading 'Paradise Lost'. I have been reading aloud from some great poem for half an hour each day. But I have also been reading missionary biography, and, oh, how it has stirred me! My heart cries out for service. I long to go!

"November 8th, 1913: My twenty-fourth birthday. I have nothing but praise and gratitude in my heart to God. My sins have been conquered and my soul is at rest. This past year has been the year of my greatest sorrow, but it has ended in victory. 'Weeping may endure for a night, but joy cometh in the morning'. And it has come, for it is morning in my soul. Oh! what fulness of joy! Christ is my sufficiency. He satisfies, for His love is eternal and unchangeable. Glory to His name!

"And now, calm and confident, I face the future. 'Dear Lord, keep me faithful. Let me burn out for Thee. Take all there is of me. Guard me from the evil one. May I dwell in Thy presence and abide in Thy love. I praise Thee for deliverance from sin, for the many opportunities of service, and for twenty-four years of life. I regret the failures and mistakes. O Lord, forgive all. I thank Thee for peace unutterable and abiding. Amen!'

"December 3rd, 1913: I have been thinking today of Heaven, for I realize that life at the longest will soon be over, and I shall go to where there will be no more unsatisfied heart-yearnings. Oh, sweet day! Take Heaven and there is nothing to live for. Life would indeed be dark and desolate. But Heaven compensates for all. I am wedded to Jesus. His love never fails. A great peace floods my heart.

"January 3rd, 1914: Spent Christmas in Toronto with my parents. Had not seen them for a year-and-a-half. A very happy visit. They have missed me greatly. Am helping them to buy their home and the payments are heavy. Preached in Dale Presbyterian Church for Rev. J. D. Morrow. A thousand present. My largest audience thus far.

"January 8th, 1914: Back in Chicago. This is what I am now striving for in my South Chicago Church:

1. *To reach the unsaved for Christ.*
2. *To turn Christians from worldliness to spirituality.*
3. *To make the prayer meeting a live service.*
4. *To build a large, enthusiastic Sunday School.*
5. *To develop a strong, missionary church.*
6. *To increase church attendance.*
7. *To put spiritual men in every office.*

"February 2nd, 1914: Oh, the joy of service! I love my work. I love preaching and teaching the blessed Word. But my greatest joy is in the transformed lives around me. God is working. Grace Armstrong has been gloriously saved. She broke down and sobbed as though her heart would break. Lydia Krueger is a new girl. And they are all testifying in public. Never have I known such happiness. These last few weeks have been, oh, so precious. The sorrow has gone. It is all sunshine. And my people—how kind they are to me!

"February 16th, 1914: Oh, that I could express the joy that was mine as a result of yesterday's work! But I never can. It was simply unspeakable. What liberty! What freedom! His power came upon me suddenly and my heart was melted. Lives, I know, were transformed.

"March 6th, 1914: Prayer meetings growing. Thirty to forty present now. Many praying who have never prayed before. Much opposition but glorious victory.

"March 13th, 1914: Finished reading Dante's 'Divine Comedy' today. Have read it aloud.

"March 25th, 1914: Received the little engagement ring back today. I am now free once more—but! We were engaged a little more than two years and four months.

"April 23rd, 1914: It was just a year ago today that the blow fell. But my heart is at rest, for since May 22nd, 1913, I have been, oh, so happy.

"May 14th, 1914: Recently I applied to the Board of Foreign Missions of the Presbyterian Church in Canada for work in the Foreign Field, but was rejected. Tried four times to go.

"June 24th, 1914: Heard Dr. F. B. Meyer, whose books have been such a blessing to me.

"During the past summer, we carried on a Union Tent Campaign and held street-meetings. Maude Sweetman was our soloist. There were 34 saved and 25 joined the Church.

"August 30th, 1914: At Winona Lake. I wrote 'Alone With Thee'. Dictated it to Myrtle Donahue.

"September 5th, 1914: Saw my first published hymns today. Music by Dr. D. B. Towner. My, what a thrill!

"September 8th, 1914: Today I finished writing the words of the hymn 'Deeper and Deeper'. The melody came to me in Woodstock, Ont., one morning, three years ago, as I was walking along the street, on my way to preach in Central Methodist Church, and it has never been changed. The words have been difficult. I have spent hours on them. But the writing of the hymn has afforded me much pleasure, and I believe it will live. I wrote it in my South Chicago Church.

"November 3rd, 1914: Have been reading the life of George Whitefield and it has set my soul aflame. His zeal, his prayer life, his preaching—how he inspires me! I now rise at 6.30 each morning and spend an hour in prayer and Bible study, and again an hour at night. And yet how ashamed I feel as I read of the fervor of Whitefield.

"November 8th, 1914: A quarter of a century of life. I am twenty-five today. This morning I read the 90th Psalm and reviewed what the Lord had done for me. Oh, how good He has been! Though delicate as a boy I have lived to this present day. For seven years I have had the privilege of preaching the Gospel! I have asked God to direct me very definitely as to my life's work, and I am praying that He will make me—

(1) *A victorious man*. (2) *A Spirit-filled man*. (3) *A man of prayer*. (4) *A man of the Word*. (5) *A surrendered man*. (6) *A man of one purpose*.

"I note from my sermon records that when I was seventeen I gave but two messages. At the age of eighteen I preached 22 times. When I was nineteen I delivered 68 addresses. At twenty 61. At twenty-one I preached 108 times. At twenty-two, 101. At twenty-three, 109. At twenty-four, 124. Hence, I have preached 595 sermons to date.

"December 7th, 1914: I have just finished reading 'With Christ in the School of Prayer', by Andrew Murray, and have been greatly blessed, especially by the word about George Muller. What a wonderful book. Oh, to be willing! I *will* go, but—will I go *willingly*?

"December 21st, 1914: At last I have heard 'Billy' Sunday, the famous Evangelist, Homer A. Rodeheaver, his Song Leader, and Chas. H. Gabriel, the noted composer. What a treat!

"December 26th, 1914: Home in Toronto. Saw Jennie to-night for the first time in nearly two years, but our engagement was not renewed, though her love has come back. She, too, has suffered much. What a mystery!

"January 15th, 1915, Chicago: Today I finished writing a choir number entitled: 'Christ is Coming Back Again'. Dr. D. B. Towner wrote the music for it.

LEAVING CHICAGO

"February 15th, 1915: Three definite Calls have come to me. Dr. Hall Young, the famous missionary explorer, wants me to go to Alaska. Rev. J. D. Morrow, to whom I applied, is anxious for me to become his Associate Pastor in Dale Presbyterian Church, Toronto. And then, of course, the members of the South Chicago Church are urging me to remain here. Juneau salary is $1,200 per year; South Chicago about the same; Toronto $600. The question is, Where does God want me? It is difficult to decide.

"Today I prayed for a long time for guidance. My soul was in agony. This evening I came to my room and once again besought God for light. Slowly the vision came to me that my work must be a world work. My own dear country seemed to call me. There must be thousands in Canada who would give their lives for missions if they could be reached. I have no preference, no will of my own. I feel with Wesley that 'the world is my parish'. Perhaps the greater opportunity is offered in the Call to Dale, although I would not look upon it as a permanent location. I must reach beyond to the world. I must travel and challenge others. May I listen to the Spirit's voice and not make a mistake. It is mine to obey orders, His to give them. But no matter where I go, may a world vision be mine.

"February 24th, 1915: God's Word came to me this morning while in class, and it was this: *'When they desired him to tarry longer time with them he consented not'* (Acts 18: 20).

And in view of the fact that the members of the South Chicago Church have gotten up a petition, signed by almost everyone, urging me to stay, I concluded that I must go to Toronto.

"April 6th, 1915: The first publication from my pen has been issued, a twelve-page tract, entitled 'The Question of Questions'. The Moody Colportage Association brought it out.

"April 29th, 1915: On Sunday, the 25th, I preached my farewell sermons in the South Chicago Presbyterian Church. And the graduating exercises of our class in McCormick Theological Seminary, were held tonight, which means the end of my student days. I have given the past five years to the study of theology.

"April 30th, 1915: Ordained tonight. I have spent the whole of this day in prayer and fasting. I read Psalms 90 and 91; John, chapters 13 and 17, as well as 1st and 2nd Timothy, and Titus. I was ordained in my own church, South Chicago Presbyterian, by the Chicago Presbytery. Rev. Henry Hepburn, D.D., Professor Hayes, Mr. Johnson, Mr. Barclay and Robert Smith, took part. Lydia Krueger and Grace Armstrong sang my hymn, 'Deeper and Deeper', and Myrtle Donahue played the organ. It was a most impressive service. The church was well filled. I am now a full-fledged Presbyterian minister."

It was not easy to leave the dear young people of South Chicago. Many of them had been saved or restored under my ministry. Never will I forget the heartache as I said goodbye. I think they felt it even more than I did. For two years we had laboured together.

During these two years I had the burden of a two-fold work, my Seminary Course and the care of the Church. The return trip across the city by street car was thirty-two miles, and I made it regularly. I preached twice each Sunday, conducted the prayer meeting on Wednesday night, taught the Bible Crusaders, and led a class in the study of Tennyson. All this in addition to visitation, funerals, business meetings, etc., and my studies in the Seminary. One time, when I was very ill, I was nursed in the home of Grace Armstrong and attended by Dr. Krueger. Through all my student days God always provided a church for me so that I never stopped preaching.

My bosom friend at McCormick was Wm. F. McDermott, who later became world-famous as a writer, especially for "The Reader's Digest" and as Religious Editor of "The Chicago News". Many a day we tramped the streets of Chicago together looking for cheap Greek restaurants. Lately he has written and published wonderful articles about my ministry.

Leaving Chicago early in May, I returned to Toronto to become Associate Pastor of Dale Presbyterian Church. I started my work on Sunday, June 6th, 1915, the year of my ordination, when I was twenty-five years of age. And I am still in Toronto. Where would I be now, I wonder, if Mr. Morrow had not accepted me? What a ministry Dale gave me! However, I knew nothing of holding great campaigns in those days and so I missed a golden opportunity. That vision came later.

CHAPTER V

DALE CHURCH

DALE PRESBYTERIAN CHURCH, TORONTO, is located at the corner of Queen Street and Bellwoods Avenue. It has a very fine auditorium with a seating capacity of eighteen hundred. For a long time it was known as "The Roofless Church", the services being held in the basement. It was built by Rev. J. D. Morrow, one of the most unique characters in Toronto. The old church, St. Mark's, had been crowded out. Hence the necessity for a new building.

During his college days Mr. Morrow was a noted athlete. He won many a trophy as a runner and held records for both Canada and the United States. He had a personal magnetism which was well nigh irresistible. His laugh was contagious and he was full of fun. He was most lovable and very friendly.

Mr. Morrow was the first man in Toronto, if not in Canada, to go without a hat. He had vowed that he would not wear a hat until he got enough money to put a roof on his church. And he kept his vow. He wore his hair long and bushy at the back and was a familiar figure on the streets of Toronto. Everybody knew him. The policemen were his friends. Each Monday morning he sat in court, watching for an opportunity to take charge of someone who had erred, whom he might bring home and help. All the street car conductors were acquainted with him. One time he borrowed a "Pay as you enter" box from the Street Car Company, and for months he and I took turns standing by it at Yonge and Shuter streets, collecting funds for his church. Sometimes he got animals from the zoo, including bears, and took them into his pulpit to attract the children. And they came in multitudes.

Moreover, he was a gifted evangelist and a most effective gospel preacher. He knew how to put on a bright, evangelistic service, and thus attract the crowds. The way he told stories,

59

actually acting them out on the platform, sang his own mother songs, and pled for decisions, always brought tears to the eyes. Many decided for Christ under his ministry. He was very active and energetic. And he was most generous. He loved the common people and never felt more at home than when among the poor. To provide for the destitute was his greatest delight. His critics were many, especially in ecclesiastical circles. He died at 48, on April 28, 1921. Had he lived he might have become one of Canada's greatest evangelists.

Never will I forget the night he first appeared with his hair cut. He had been made Chaplain of the Sportsman's Battalion, the 180th, and was dressed in the uniform of a Captain. For a long time he hesitated behind the curtain. Finally he told me to go first. I stepped out and he followed. In a moment the great congregation burst into applause.

When the time came for him to speak he took as his text, "So then each one of us shall give account of himself to God," and preached with all his old-time fire, pausing in the midst of his sermon to sing a verse of his favourite song, "Where is my Wandering Boy Tonight?" Speaking again, and then singing the second verse, as the choir led by "Sandy" Grant, came in softly on the chorus, he made his appeal. Handkerchiefs were used freely throughout the congregation. A woman wept aloud. In the gallery a man bowed his head and sobbed as though his heart would break. Oh, what power!

Such was the man who accepted me as his Associate Pastor. Already he had meant much to me. I owe him a debt that I can never hope to pay, for he it was who gave me my start. He took me at the age of twenty-five and allotted me an equal share with him in his great work. We preached alternately every Sunday, morning and night, and we always had a full house. The basement held a thousand, but frequently we packed in as many as twelve hundred eager listeners. And to that enthusiastic audience I had the privilege of preaching for nearly four years while still in my twenties. Think of it! To go direct from Seminary to a large city church. What a miracle!

I started on $600 a year. At the end of six months my salary was raised to $1,000. It was paid by Knox Presbyterian Church, where Rev. A. B. Winchester, D.D., was the minister. During the same year, 1915, I was made President of the Alumni Association of the Toronto Bible College. In those days we wore the now out-dated long Prince Albert coat.

My first year at Dale was a year of trial and sickness. However, "I sought the Lord and He heard me." F. B. Meyer's booklets were greatly blessed to my soul, and before the year was out I had entered into a new life of victory and blessing. On July 12th, 1915, I took Jennie canoeing during the evening on the Humber. It was our final meeting.

As a result of reading the biography of Robert Murray Mc-Cheyne, The New Acts of the Apostles, and Quo Vadis, I became greatly burdened for revival and missions. I began attending a four o'clock prayer-meeting which was held every Friday at the West End Y.M.C.A., where a number of ministers and laymen met to pray for revival, among them, Dr. E. Ralph Hooper. Never will I forget those meetings. They were like a breath from Heaven. Mr. G. N. Elliott was then secretary.

"God is speaking to me," I wrote in my diary. "The missionary life of sacrifice and suffering for Christ sets my heart throbbing with emotion. Oh, the joy of service! If I cannot be a missionary abroad, I must be one at home. Truly, the supreme task of the church is the evangelization of the world. Missionary work does not belong to any one organization; it is the work of the whole church."

Dale Church was formally opened on April 2nd, 1916. Miss Daisy Billings, Mr. Morrow's deaconess, who had come to Dale nearly two years before, had preached the final sermon in the basement on the preceding Sunday. I was very ill and could not be present, but I was told that she preached to a tremendous crowd and made a deep impression. Soon after the opening day I left for Clifton Springs, New York, where I remained for some time, recuperating.

ENGAGED AND MARRIED

During May, 1916, I spent much time looking for a house, and finally found a little bungalow at 58 Garden Avenue, which I bought on easy terms for $4,000. Before closing the deal I took Miss Billings through it to see whether or not it would appeal to her. She was delighted with it. That was before we were engaged.

For years I had offered up two petitions, one, that God

would give me a work after His own heart, and the other, that He would give me a helpmate after His own heart. We were engaged on May 26th, 1916.

Before coming to Dale as deaconess, Miss Billings had worked among the mountaineers of Virginia, after leaving Nyack where she had taken her Bible training. Her home was in Peterborough. Mr. Morrow greatly admired her and spoke of her as the best deaconess in all Canada. Hearts were always moved when she preached, for she was greatly beloved. She had many qualities of refinement and was deeply spiritual. She knew from experience the meaning of the word "sacrifice".

On June 2nd, 1916, on the banks of the Humber, where we had spent an evening canoeing, we sealed our engagement with a ring. And as we prayed together, we knew that God had satisfied our hearts, and that He would bless our united lives. Poems expressing deep joy, gratitude and love, such as "Only a Ring," were born out of that sacred experience. In my diary I compared myself to a man looking for gold and finding a nugget. She has been the very essence of faithfulness and loyalty.

Together we bought things for our little home, and together we placed them in the various rooms. She seemed to know exactly how to arrange everything. Her taste was excellent. I soon discovered that with her I was going to have a real home. No wonder we were happy.

We were married on September 12th, 1916, on the platform of Dale Church. Rev. J. D. Morrow, assisted by Rev. John McNicol, B.D., performed the ceremony. The church was packed to the door, some 2,000 being present, with hundreds on the outside. Somehow the taxi driver got the wrong number and the bride was over half an hour late. As we left the church we were showered with rice and confetti, while several policemen cleared a passage through the cheering crowd.

Contrary to the expectations of all we went straight to our little home at 58 Garden Avenue. We had been granted passes on the railway to Quebec for our honeymoon, and all thought we were going at once. In fact, Mr. Morrow went down to the station and right through the pullmans calling out my name and all the time we were resting quietly at home. For several days we remained in Toronto unknown to anyone, and then, finally, left for our wedding trip to old Quebec. Having no money, I borrowed $50 for our honeymoon. Large pictures of us appeared in the evening papers.

My salary was now raised to $1,500 per year. On October 16th, 1916, I was placed in full charge of Dale, Mr. Morrow having to leave for the Front. What an honour! Dale was one of the largest Presbyterian churches in the whole of Canada, and I was only 26 years of age.

Contrary to the predictions of many, the crowds in Dale Church began to increase. But, of course, Satan got busy at once. There was much strife in the choir and in the session. "The mixed multitude" was greatly in evidence. I was hampered by the lodge. Officials were elected because of their lodge affiliation. Worldliness calmoured for recognition.

But God gave us one truly born-again man, a Mr. Wm. J. Hutchinson, who became the superintendent of our Sunday School. He was a real help to me all through those trying days, for he stood for a saved choir. Then, too, after much heated debate, I secured Dr. and Mrs. M. W. Lau as my assistants. Miss Alice Porter became my deaconess on January 1st, 1918.

On June 22nd, 1917, God blessed our home with the birth of a son. Glen Gilmour, we named him. Dr. E. Ralph Hooper was the attending physician. Long before his birth we had solemnly dedicated him to God. Thus we were united anew and we were very happy at 58 Garden Avenue though we passed through numerous trials, mostly of a financial nature. Some months later, my wife was seriously ill, but God undertook for her. Sometimes we had no money for coal and had to let the furnace go out, even in the coldest weather, and sleep in the kitchen.

A MYSTERIOUS EXPERIENCE

One of the most mysterious experiences of my life happened about this time. I am not going to try to explain it. I give it for what it is worth.

A very fine woman, Mrs. Charman by name, was ill in Edmonton. So low was she that the beat of her heart could not be detected. In her unconsciousness she had a most remarkable vision. She was in deep darkness. But just ahead of her she saw a light, brighter, it seemed, than a thousand suns. And as she watched, she heard music, the unutterable music of Heaven.

In the distance she saw a boy about sixteen years of age, with fair hair and blue eyes. And as she looked he pled with her to come to the light.

At last, to the amazement of all, she opened her eyes, and in due time recovered. From then on she sought for the boy of her vision, for she was convinced that she would one day meet him. Later the family moved to Winnipeg. Frequently when on the street cars she would eagerly scan the faces of the passengers.

"What are you looking for?" her daughter would ask her.

"The boy," was her reply.

They moved to Toronto, and still she sought for the face she had seen in the vision.

One day she was sitting in Trinity Park opposite Dale Church. The congregation was singing "I Need Thee Every Hour" and the music thrilled her. She was reminded of the heavenly strains she had heard in her vision. Something seemed to draw her and the following Sunday she was present. When the time came to start the service I walked out and sat down behind the pulpit as usual. She gave one long, startled look and then turned pale.

"Mother's fainting," exclaimed her daughter, alarmed.

Recovering, she looked again. Yes, the same face, light hair, blue eyes, the boy of her vision, now some nine years older. When I spoke she recognised the voice in a moment. It was the voice of the boy calling her to the light. And oh, how marvellously the light broke for her. She became one of my greatest intercessors. Day and night she prayed for revival. Now she is with her Lord. But oh, how wonderfully Mrs. Charman's prayers have been answered!

MY NEW BURDEN

Dated July 27th, 1917, my diary contains the following entry: "The seriousness of my Calling has been impressed upon me more than ever of late. The fact that I have been chosen of God for a specific ministry and that I have been responsible for the faithful discharge of that ministry, has come home to me with tremendous force. Men are perishing all around me and their only hope is Christ; hence they must be saved or they will be lost eternally. The great truths concerning Sin and Salvation, Heaven, Hell and Judgment have gripped my heart. I am here on business for my King, and if I am not here for business, I have no business to be here.

"The reason for this new burden has been the reading of the great works of the Puritans, given to me by Samuel Stevenson, with whom I spent many hours in prayer. Oh, what mighty preachers they were! Joseph Alleine's 'An Alarm to Unconverted Sinners', Richard Baxter's 'A Call to the Unconverted', and John Angell James' 'The Anxious Inquirer After Salvation'—these are the books. 'I will spend the day for eternity,' writes Joseph Alleine. 'May it be your whole study to gain souls, and to build them up in holiness'."

(From this point, August 16th, 1917, to the latter part of September, 1918, my Diary will be found in the latter part of my book, "The Passion for Souls". Hence these entries are omitted here. I would suggest that the book be secured and this important part read before continuing, so as not to break the record. Suffice it to say that we experienced a breath of old-time revival that reminded us of many of the experiences of Chas. G. Finney. Deep conviction, glorious salvation and abounding joy characterized our meetings. There were many decisions for Christ.)

It was during this time that "A Revival Hymn" was born. Mrs. Charman prophesied that it would one day be sung around the world. Today it looks as though her prediction might be fulfilled.

Mr. Morrow returned on March 28th, 1918, and on Sunday the 31st he and I faced the largest audience we had ever seen in Dale. There must have been nearly 3,000 packed in. I had charge and Mr. Morrow spoke. But let me quote from "The Globe":

"Storms of hand clapping greeted Captain Morrow when he rose to speak. Time after time his remarks were punctuated by applause. The reception accorded him was magnificent. All seating space in the church was occupied long before the service commenced and hundreds crowded into a room at the top of the building, the windows of which looked over the auditorium. Six people fainted and had to be removed. One of the ladies in the choir burst into repeated cries of, 'Oh, my brother! my brother! my brother!' and collapsed, still sobbing out the phrase. The audience caught its breath and men

c

as well as women could be seen weeping. The moment was tense."

On May 28th, 1918, I heard the world famous Gipsy Smith for the first time. What an inspiration! Little did I know then that he would later become a bosom friend.

During August, 1918, we re-visited Embro and the scenes of my boyhood days, the first time in seven years. I found that the old station in which we had lived had been moved a mile west, only the trees we had planted remaining to mark the spot, and they, too, are now gone. We saw again the little red school house at Cody's Corners, and poor old Mrs. Sutherland, who soon recognised me and was overjoyed. Gently she stroked little Glen's face. Dr. Green, Florence Sharpe and others, welcomed us back. Osborne McKenzie had been killed in the war.

In September I was much helped by Wm. R. Newell, who taught me the wonderful truth of freedom from the law; in other words, that it is not because God forbids, but because Christ indwells and sets us free, that we obey. Later I raised the first $1,100.00 toward the publication of Mr. Newell's now well known book on "Romans".

FAREWELL TO DALE

On October 27th, 1918, I preached my farewell sermon in Dale Church, having resigned after a hard and bitter fight. The praying people stood with me. Countless hours were spent pleading with God. Dr. Hooper, Miss Porter, Mrs. Charman, Mr. Stevenson and others held on to God for victory to the end. But some of the officials and the worldly members of the congregation were against me. Knox Church backed me and withdrew their annual grant of $1,500 when I left.

I had caused offence by raising over $600 for Missions. My revival meetings were a constant source of irritation. There was a strong objection taken to the gospel hymns we were singing and the many prayer meetings we were holding. We were constantly referred to as "Mr. Smith and his soul-saving gang". Unfortunately, I had been influenced to take sides and, in a moment of discouragement, I handed in my resignation.

I was still in my twenties, and being young and inexperienced, I felt I should give in and resign rather than remain and fight. Had I been more of a diplomat I might have pleased both factions. I was crushed and broken-hearted. Our sufferings were intense. Many were stricken, and bitter, bitter tears were shed. But now that it is over and God has more than vindicated, it would be useless to re-open the old sores and uncover the past. May my ministry of three and a half precious years in Dale Church, with all its failures and mistakes, its revival blessings and victories, redound to His glory in that great Day!

On November 5th, 1918, my diary records the fact that I was officially received into the Presbytery of Toronto, and given my full standing as a minister of the Presbyterian Church of Canada, from which I have never resigned, although my work ever since leaving Dale has been, for the most part, outside the denomination.

The following excerpt from my diary is worth noting: "November 8th, 1918. My twenty-ninth birthday. This is a solemn year for me. It was at the age of twenty-nine that both David Brainerd and Robert Murray McCheyne died, after having been mightily used of God. I too would gladly lay down my life if only my eyes could see the power and glory of God in a mighty revival. But I am afraid there is still far too much of self. God help me! How I need Him!"

During this time I received much help from Dr. Charles G. Trumbull, who held a Victorious Life Conference, and also from Paul Rader, who conducted a great soul-winning campaign in Massey Hall. I literally sang for joy as I walked the street in His victory.

In the Rader campaign I was greatly humbled. At first I ushered, but was soon set aside. Then I tried to do personal work, but was ignored. Finally I sold hymn books in the aisles, while Dr. Hooper and other leaders occupied seats on the platform. God knows, I needed to be broken, but oh, how I suffered! Years later I myself had the joy of bringing Paul Rader to Toronto and to Massey Hall. It was during this campaign (January 29th to February 5th, 1919) that my hymn "Saved" was introduced by Mr. Rader's Song Leader, Arthur W. McKee.

For some months I was pastor of Beulah Tabernacle (Central Hall), and as opportunity offered, preached and won souls in halls, churches and missions. I was offered the pastorate of St. Clarens Ave. Church at a salary of $1,600, but refused it. Wm. R. Newell wanted me to travel with him as an evangelist. Of course, I should have gone at once to the Presbyterian Church and asked for another charge, but I never thought of it and no one ever suggested it to me. However, if I had, I might have been sent to some little country town and my voice never heard. Whereas God wanted me in Toronto.

CHAPTER VI

THE CALL OF THE WILD

A T ONE of Paul Rader's meetings, Mr. Wm. Henderson, Founder and Superintendent of the Shantymen's Christian Association, said something to me about the need of a man to open up the work in British Columbia. That day I thought no more about it, but next morning while in prayer, his suggestion came back to me. I stopped praying, told my wife, and then 'phoned Mr. Henderson. Thus a Presbyterian minister became a lumberjack preacher.

On March 21st, 1919, with Mrs. Smith and our little Glen, I boarded the train for my second trip to the far West. Passing through Chicago, I met once again the dear converts and workers of the South Chicago Presbyterian Church, after four years' absence. Poor Grace I found ill with tuberculosis. She is now with Christ. Oh, what memories! Finally, by way of Winnipeg, we reached British Columbia, where I visited once more friends and scenes of eleven years before. Again I saw Hartley Bay, Prince Rupert and Fort Simpson.

Yes, eleven years had passed since, at the age of 18, I had worked among the Indians, and I was now in British Columbia again. Altogether I made seven missionary journeys up the coast. I was joined in my work by Messrs. William Henderson, Alex. Weir, Jim Matheson, and Dr. E. Ralph Hooper. We travelled by steamer, launch, logging train and by canoe and boat. Frequently we walked the boom.

THRILLING EXPERIENCES

My diary contains many descriptions of our thrilling experiences and narrow escapes as we rode the logging trains through mountainous scenery, more beautiful than Switzerland, in order to preach the Gospel to those who did not want it and who only persecuted us for our pains. It was a life of

indescribable excitement in the great open spaces of a new
world. But let me quote from my diary:

"May 13th: For many miles this rough mountain railway,
following the river's course, wound in and out, up and down,
over high trestle work, that rivals the C.P.R. across the
Rockies. One rises up perpendicular from which one could
dive into eight hundred feet of water. The mountain lakes are
very deep. And oh, how beautiful they are, these little bodies
of fresh water that nestle among the mighty peaks. Here is a
veritable Paradise for the fishermen, for they teem with trout.
From the top of a lofty peak it is possible to count some twenty
of these lakes.

"It took us some time to get used to riding on the logging
trains, for it is a nerve-racking experience at first. Standing on
a platform some six feet by ten, whirled along at a rapid rate
of speed, around curves and over trestles, through unbroken
forests that stand in all their primeval grandeur, now tearing
up a steep grade, now down a rapid incline, the engine snorting and puffing, a man at every brake ready for any emergency—such is the rather novel experience of riding on a logging train.

"May 16th: We walked to a camp this morning, stopping
on our way to watch them loading logs. What a sight it is!—
the donkey engine snorting and puffing as it winds up the great
cable with three or four logs attached, drawing them along the
skid-road from a quarter of a mile away: then with a great
hook in each end of a large log attached to a cable running
through a pulley away up at the top of an upright, well cabled
on every side, hauling the log up in the air, swinging it around
like some giant living thing, holding it suspended over the car
until it swings into position, then dropping it suddenly at a
given signal, into place. If it does not fall exactly right, it
leaps again into the air, like a living monster, and then
plunges once more into position.

"May 30th: Our voyage this afternoon in a small rowboat
was rather perilous. The waves were high, the boat frail, and
there were three of us in it. Unable to make the shore, we were
forced to land on the boom, and a dangerous landing it was. A
small raft was fastened to it over which the waves rushed two
feet high in quick succession. It tossed like a shell on the great
deep, while the logs heaved and sank with the violence of the
water that poured over them. Our boat should have been

smashed against the raft, but it wasn't. How we got out I don't know, but we did. To slip off a log would mean being crushed to death between. But by stepping quickly from one to another we at last gained the shore and were once more safe in camp. It was surely the Lord who preserved us.

RESCUED BY INDIANS

"July 21st: At noon today Dr. Hooper and I asked the Manager about the possibilities of getting away by boat. He ignored us, and we saw that we were held in utter contempt.

"In the woods we prayed and finally there flashed into our minds the memory of an Indian village some two miles up the river. To this village, past the camp, along the river and through the woods we made our way, but we were on the wrong side. Across the river a boy and girl were having a hilarious time in the water. We called to them and in a moment the boy had donned a pair of trousers and with swift strokes was on our side.

"When he had rowed us over we found an old Indian woman drying some salmon in the sun. After a good deal of palaver in Chinook and English we made an agreement with her to take us to the wharf in her dug-out for $2.00. The village was deserted for the most part as the Indians were away fishing, but she found an old man who took the stern, and, with the boy at the prow, we started. Right past the camp we paddled and, finally, arrived at the wharf after a trip of about four miles. God used the Indians to do for us what our own white people should have done, but would not. Thus the way was opened for us to get out of the camp when everything seemed to be completely blocked. We held a meeting tonight on the floating wharf with hearts full of joy and gratitude to God for the wonderful deliverance which He wrought on our behalf.

"July 28th: We had a long weary trudge to the boat twelve miles away. Arriving at the beach, we found all the beds full, and it was now after midnight. However, we discovered a pile of mattresses, and, dragging four of them out to the edge of the Ocean, we laid one on the ground, placed two across and bound these two together by another, then crawled under the third, and, in no time at all, lost consciousness. It was one of the most delightful rests we had had.

"August 18th: Dr. Hooper had not spoken long until someone in the camp started the gasoline saw, and while an ordinary crosscut saw is bad enough, it is nothing compared with the noises made by one run by a gasoline engine, but the Doctor went on speaking. Then someone began to cut wood with an axe and a great sledge hammer, which added to the difficulty. Finally, when neither of these noises sufficed to stop the preaching, the engineer went down and turned on the steam locomotive standing near by, and then, of course, it was impossible for our voices to be heard.

"August 26th: We obtained a promise from the Superintendent to take us back on the speeder after our meeting, and, with carefree hearts, we prepared for our return trip. But when we got to the office we were informed that the speeder had already left. It had been done deliberately: we saw that in a moment, for a number of the men had gathered around to see how we would take our disappointment. We expressed no anxiety whatever, but quietly prepared for our long trudge on foot.

"With hearty farewells and many expressions of thanks, we started for the Beach, twelve miles away. Long before we had crossed the last of the seven great trestles our legs ached, but at every step we praised the Lord, 'rejoicing that we were counted worthy to suffer shame for His Name'."

The camps were filled with Bolsheviks who bitterly opposed us. At one time a giant of a lumberjack called me out to beat me up but God delivered me out of his hands. We slept in the bunkhouses and ate with the men. Some 35,000 tracts were distributed. Much of the time we preached in the open-air, often with no-one in sight, but we knew that scores were listening behind closed doors. It reminded me of the ministry of Wesley and Whitefield.

Thus I spent the Summer of 1919. Dr. E. Ralph Hooper had left his splendid practice in Toronto to accompany me, a practice to which he never returned; the rest of his life being spent in full-time Christian service. It was an unforgettable experience. Thus the work of the Shantymen's Christian Association was launched in British Columbia, a work that has continued ever since.

CHAPTER VII

THE GOSPEL AUDITORIUM

I T WAS in British Columbia, at a place called Jackson Bay,
Dr. E. Ralph Hooper, a successful Christian physician
from Toronto, and I, as already recorded, had left our
homes in Old Ontario to preach the Gospel to the lumbermen
of the Pacific Coast. It was our habit to retire into the great
forests that covered the mountain slopes and pour out our
hearts in prayer for God's blessing upon our work.

On this special afternoon, July 11th, 1919, we had made
our way along the coast to a spot about a mile or more from
the camp. A large tree had fallen across a gully, and it was
on that tree that we knelt that day to wrestle with God in
prayer. High above us the great mountains rose in magnificent
splendour on every side. Behind us the forest in all its primeval
glory made a most picturesque background; while a few feet
away the ever restless ocean swells broke upon the lonely
shore. Across the bay there stood a small cabin in which lived
a woman and her daughter, isolated from the great world
outside. We were far away from civilization, kneeling amid
the grandeur of God's handiwork.

Never will I forget that day. For while we prayed, as
recorded in my diary: "God came very near. The impression
came to me with much joy and exaltation of spirit that I was
to return to Toronto. I saw in vision the needy souls, and my
heart went out to them. Perhaps it is to start an independent
work on faith lines, I cannot say, but I am willing for whatever He wants."

It was an unmistakable Call. The whole work seemed to
open up before me. I saw myself as the shepherd of the
people, and I felt certain that God had a work for me there,
though we were then more than 3,000 miles away. My heart
rejoiced within me, and rising from my knees, I left the Doctor
and went a little farther along the shore, praying and praising
by turns, unable to restrain my feelings.

73

At another time, while praying the prayer of Paul: "Lord, what wilt Thou have me to do?" I received the answer, as noted in my diary under August 27th, 1919: "Arise, and go into the city, and it shall be told thee what thou must do" (Acts 9: 6). And one night while pacing back and forth on the stern of the vessel that was carrying us to civilization, I saw myself in vivid imagination in Toronto calling the people back to God. Thus, there could be no choice but to return. And so in the fall of the same year, with my wife and Glen, and Miss Alice Porter, who had been visiting us, by boat and train via Prince Rupert, I came back.

BACK IN TORONTO

Full of expectation and confidence, I once more found myself in Toronto. For a few days I waited upon God in prayer and then left for a week's work among the lumber camps in Northern Ontario.

Then I waited, but little did I know how long I would have to wait, for that whole winter passed, and also the following summer before the vision was fulfilled. I was now in the school of God learning patience; and, oh, what a blessed thing it is to wait on Him. At times I would walk around the district looking at the houses and wondering when God's time would come. I called it "viewing the walls".

Toward the close of winter I was walking the floor, praying, when I received a definite impression of a hall at Queen and Dovercourt. I did not know of any, but I immediately put on my hat and coat and walked down to make sure. It was there. It was the old West End Y.M.C.A. I made enquiries, found that there were 750 seats, and that the rent was $25.00 a night.

On the way home this word came to me: "Behold, I have set before thee an open door and no man can shut it", which I took to mean that God would keep it free for me until His time came. Not a word did I say to anyone. I was upbraided for my inactivity, for I was earning only $15.00 a week assisting Rev. R. V. Bingham with the editing of "The Evangelical Christian", working half time. I went to prayer and rehearsed it all before the Lord. Two or three times I tried to find a way out by securing a Pastorate, but without success.

But, oh, how hard it was! What a different life I was now leading! Once, a busy Pastor, ministering to multitudes, now, alone, shut in with God. He had to teach me that "It is a good thing that a man both hope and quietly wait for the salvation of the Lord".

On December 11th, 1919, I saw a copy of my first book of poems, a beautiful cloth-bound volume, but was compelled to destroy the entire edition because the publisher objected to some of the poems. Will I ever forget it?

This from my Diary: "January 1st, 1920: There has come into my heart a desire to have a spiritual work where souls will be saved and sent out as missionaries and the people trained to give to missions."

On February 4th, 1920, God gave us our one and only daughter, Hope Evangeline. She was born at 6 Muir Avenue, when Glen and I were both dangerously sick with the flu. Our whole family, like many others, might have been wiped out at that time, for I had a fearful relapse.

In March I wrote the appeals in "The Globe" for the Armenians and over a quarter-of-a-million dollars came in. They paid me $50.00. (Story in "Tales of the Mission Field".)

At the end of May, with Dr. Hooper, I returned to Cawood, Kentucky, to preach, where I had last ministered as a student in 1913, but only remained a month. The Doctor was taken seriously ill and I had to bring him back to Canada on a kitchen chair. However, we held 64 services in 25 days and saw 42 decisions. We visited 500 homes. Thus was launched the work of the Shantymen's Christian Association in Kentucky, a work that continued for many years.

On Thursday morning, August 26th, I was praying. Presently, there stole into my heart a new confidence, an inexpressible fullness of faith, and I knew that God's time had come. I had waited a year and a half. The conviction now came to me that the work of The Gospel Auditorium, as I had decided to call it, was to be launched on the first Sunday of October, 1920. I had been definitely booked for two engagements, but I prayed about them and both were broken, and as I faced my new venture, my heart was filled with unutterable peace.

Without saying a word to a soul, I began asking God for the necessary money for the rent. Three days later Mr. W. W. Sneath handed Dr. Hooper $10.00 for me. Each day Dr.

Hooper and I met for prayer, but I gave him no hint as to what I was about to do. God's Word was unspeakably precious to me, especially that word "wait". "My soul, wait thou only upon God, for my expectation is from Him." Again and again He spoke to me.

I read "The Life of Trust", by George Muller, and was greatly encouraged as I pored over its 545 pages. Sixteen days later I spent two hours in prayer and, in the afternoon, had an unexpected wedding, the first for almost a year, and got $5.00. That night I prayed for money in the morning mail, something I had never experienced before, and, next morning, got a cheque for $5.00 from a Mr. Moses.

A few days before the first Sunday of October I opened my mail—it was on a Thursday afternoon—and found a cheque for $15.00 from Mr. W. H. Adamson. I fairly shouted for joy. He sent me the following letter: "I awoke some time during the night and a message—no doubt from God—came to me: 'Send Oswald Smith some money'." So the day of miracles had not passed. The Holy Spirit was still able to speak to a Christian business man. I now had $60.00. God had set to His seal and at last I informed Dr. Hooper. On Friday he and I went from door to door distributing dodgers.

Three weeks earlier I had written out the following Constitution:

ORIGIN—Born of God on the 1st Sunday of October, 1920, after almost fifteen months of continuous waiting upon Him in definite believing prayer, in response to an unmistakable Call.

PURPOSE—First—A testimony to the faithfulness of God and the reliability of His promises, that He may be glorified. Second—The salvation of souls, the edification of believers, and world-wide evangelism.

METHODS—First—A work of faith, wholly dependent upon God. Its needs are brought to Him in prayer, and to Him alone. Second—No collections are taken up and no solicitations for funds authorized. Third—No debts are incurred, the work being enlarged only as the Lord indicates His will by sending in the means. Fourth—One-tenth of the total income is set aside for Missions.

THE DAY ARRIVES

At last the day of days arrived. Never will I forget it. I got there at 6.00 p.m. No one was going in. With a sinking heart I viewed the 750 empty seats, then, stealing behind a door, I knelt and prayed, and, as I prayed, I watched through the crack to see if anyone was coming. At last two men appeared. They hurried to the gallery, thinking, I suppose, that it would be filled. Finally sixty-five gathered and I preached.

Mr. Howard S. Wade was my pianist. Mr. Wm. J. Hutchinson took over the Children's Services, and Miss A. Moffat became my Bible Woman, each in dependence upon God. Mr. and Mrs. Hall made me a pulpit, and Mr. B. L. Mullen presented me with two boxes for freewill offerings.

Soon I received invitations that would have taken me away, but I turned them down. Then I was prostrated with a severe illness. But I knew God was with me and I never doubted.

On the third Sunday I needed $25.00 to pay the rent. That morning I preached in Olivet Church. Mr. A. G. Malcolm, who was present, sent me a cheque for $50.00, and I paid the rent. Later, he became one of my greatest supporters. He is now with Christ.

On the fourth Sunday I needed $4.82 to pay the rent. I received $5.00 in Monday morning's mail (anonymous). On the fifth Sunday I needed $11.02. I found $11.66 in the free-will box, 64c to the good. How wonderful of God!

November 18th I had nothing for the newspaper announcements. Friday morning's mail brought me a $5.00 bill, just what I needed. Later on, when I again lacked money for the rent, after praying for several days, I received a money order from Dr. Hooper for $10.00. Thus the Lord worked and yet no one had ever been asked for a cent, nor had I made my needs known. The income for October was $191.00, and one tenth was sent to Faith Missions.

For ourselves I took nothing except what was definitely designated for our personal use. "Lord," I cried, in the agony of my soul, "I have nothing, nothing but Thee." Yet He did not permit me to doubt. Now, see what happened! On Friday, October 22nd, Miss E. Whitehead handed me an envelope with $10.00 marked "For Your Personal Use". This was God's seal and my heart was filled with praise.

During September we received $27.50 for our own personal

use. For October, $31.25. These were months of trial and testing. A little had to go a long way, for the War was on and everything was high. Moreover, I had a wife and two children to keep. During November God was very good. We received $68.33. December was the best of all. He gave us $112.50. Thus the amount was increased each month. How I praised Him!

And so for the three never-to-be-forgotten months the Lord enabled me to carry on the work of The Gospel Auditorium, and never had His presence been more real. Finally, this peculiar form of testing came to an end, but the vision was yet to be fulfilled.

CHAPTER VIII

THE ALLIANCE TABERNACLE

ONE day, late in December, 1920, there came in my mail a copy of "The Alliance Weekly", with a picture of Dr. A. B. Simpson, founder of the Christian and Missionary Alliance, on the front page. As I stood looking at it, God seemed to say to me, "This is your work."

After waiting upon Him in prayer, I conferred with Rev. A. W. Roffe, the Canadian Superintendent, and the work of The Gospel Auditorium was amalgamated with that of Parkdale Tabernacle, 1239 Queen Street West. On the first Sunday of January, 1921, I was installed as Pastor.

I realized at the time that I was not to remain permanently in that location. I knew there would be a further development, and I planned accordingly. Parkdale had decided to close for good just before I came. Less than two dozen were attending, yet I accepted it. How God had humbled me!

Three-and-a-half months after I took charge, the Bosworth Brothers were brought to the City by the Head Office. For the first week the meetings were held in Parkdale Tabernacle. So large were the audiences that every night, without a single exception, the doors had to be closed and many were turned away. At the beginning of the second week the services were transferred to Massey Hall, seating 3,400, but, on several occasions, even Massey Hall proved inadequate to hold the crowds. There was a great deal of newspaper publicity.

So great was the interest that I decided to continue the special meetings even after the Bosworth Brothers had left, and so, for six months, every night in the week, services were held, special speakers being brought to the city week after week. For a month-and-a-half the week-day services were in Parkdale Tabernacle and the Sunday evening meetings in Massey Hall, for which there was a rental of $100.00 per night, but there were no difficulties so far as finances were concerned. Fred L. Syme became our Soloist and Song Leader.

It was at this time, June 1, 1921, at 6 Muir Ave., that Paul Brainerd, our youngest son, was born, who, though frail and delicate was destined to sing and preach the Gospel to multitudes around the world, and to become, first, the Associate Pastor and then the Pastor of The Peoples Church. From the time he was five until he was twelve he sang in my meetings and was written up in the newspapers as the Golden Voiced Soloist. His singing of "I'm Going Higher" in the great Trinity Auditorium, Los Angeles, and The Peoples Church, Toronto, has never been forgotten. His deep, full voice easily reached the 2,000 people.

Finally, we erected a large tent, 90 feet square, on the north side of College Street, near Spadina, at a cost of $2,000. We opened the tent by announcing a Chair Shower with the words, "Bring Your Own Chair," and from all parts of the city, the chairs poured in, until the tent was entirely seated. It was dedicated by Paul Rader on Sunday morning, July 3rd, 1921. The news of the work hit the Movement like a bombshell.

From the very first we were sure that God had given us the hearts of the people. They came in multitudes. Many times the edge of the platform and hastily constructed plank seats had to be utilized, though even then scores were compelled to stand. It was a time of rich spiritual blessing when many found Christ and were led into a life of victory over sin.

My own heart was filled with enthusiasm, for it was all so new to me and I was enjoying it immensely. It was the beginning of a new and enlarged ministry. I was now thirty-one years of age. God had used the Bosworth Brothers to give me a fresh start and to show me how to hold campaigns. My vision was to be fulfilled and my prayers answered.

A NEW WORK

We were now confronted with the problem of erecting a new Tabernacle, and, little by little, the money began to come in. We received $1,000.00 in Victory Bonds, and a Diamond Ring. Then we were offered a cheque for $5,000.00 for the Building Fund or a house for a manse. We took the former. Someone gave us a Victory Bond worth $500.00 with which to buy a car, but it also went into the Building Fund. Later Mr. S. A. Conklin presented us with a new car. Finally, we held a half-day of prayer and, at the close, Mr. George R. Gregg placed $15,000.00 at our disposal.

At last we chose a site on Christie Street overlooking Willow-vale Park, which we purchased, and, on it, built a steel Tabernacle 80 feet by 130 feet, costing—including the furnishings—$40,000.00. We felt that we should not waste God's money in a beautiful church building, and let Missions suffer. We provided no Sunday School or Young People's rooms—just a large, plain auditorium, into which to gather the Christless masses for a great soul-winning effort, a choir loft, book-room and pastor's study, so that, with a corps of ushers and personal workers, we would be able to hold evangelistic campaigns and reach the multitudes for God. That was my vision. Mr. W. C. Willis, one of my closest friends, was Chairman of the work. The dedication Services were held by Paul Rader on Sunday, May 14th, 1922, when we received, in cash and pledges, an additional amount of $5,000.00. Paul Rader was a great inspiration to me.

Great crowds started attending immediately. Again and again the Tabernacle was filled to over-flowing, numbers being compelled to stand. Sometimes scores of faces were seen gazing through the open windows in the summer time. The Cleveland Quintet, Clark and Bell, and scores of others ministered.

Nor did God fail us financially. No mortgage was ever placed on the Tabernacle. The first payment fell due on October 16th and on Sunday, following two half nights of prayer, a cash offering was received of $3,100.00, which more than covered both principal and interest. The last payment, which amounted to $3,745.00, fell due six months later and the offering received in actual cash on Sunday was $4,090.70, with additional pledges, payable in thirty days, of $759.00, nearly $1,100.00 more than required. What an answer to prayer! Thus, within a year and a half, the Tabernacle was free of debt.

Satan, too, was busy. There were those who opposed and who were judged. One man threatened to sue us for several thousand dollars, but our Committee prayed and God delivered.

There were many developments. We organized, for instance, The Tabernacle Publishers and sold thousands of dollars' worth of books. Then, too, The Wayside Mission was organized and workers sent out two by two to preach the Gospel in our Canadian North Land. A publication was launched, which later became "The Peoples Magazine", and it was widely circulated. Then, too, The King's Messengers, namely, tract distributors, were put to work, and almost 100,000 tracts were distributed in a single year. A "House of Seekers After Truth" was founded, to reach the Jews, with Ex-Rabbi Henry Bregman in charge, and for some thirteen years, a magnificent testimony was given. Later, in co-operation with the district, The Canadian Bible Institute was launched in a new building adjoining the Tabernacle, with Dr. E. Ralph Hooper, B.A., as its Principal, and many young people, who are now in the Foreign Field, were trained. It was later moved to Regina, Sask.

Most gratifying of all was the increase in missionary offerings. The following were the amounts given year by year: $3,693, $5,630, $10,323, $16,756, $22,793, $34,000, a total of $93,195.

BEGINNING A WORLD MINISTRY

As a result of the work of The Alliance Tabernacle, calls began to come from various parts of the United States and Canada, and from that time I started leaving Toronto and my work to hold special meetings in other places. This was the beginning of a great world-wide ministry. I went in 1921 to St. John, N.B., and Halifax, N.S. Then in 1923 Binghampton, New York, and later to Brooklyn and other places.

It was in 1923 that I received a unanimous Call from The Gospel Tabernacle, New York, to succeed Dr. A. B. Simpson, founder of the C. & M.A., as pastor of that important work, and I almost decided to accept. Mrs. A. B. Simpson, who was present, was very anxious for me to come. She felt, so she said, that I had both her husband's vision and message. But one Saturday night, October 18th, while in bed praying about it, this word came to me, "Seekest thou great things for thyself? Seek them not. I, the Lord, am mighty. I will exalt thee in due time," and in a moment my decision was reversed. And now "What hath God wrought!"

The Gospel Tabernacle was "the mother church of the Alliance," and when this important Call came, I was only 33 years of age. The property, which was downtown in New York, was then valued at half a million dollars. They wanted to sell it, and, under my leadership, build a much larger auditorium in a residential district of the city, to be known as the "Simpson Memorial Church." This, of course, was never done since I did not accept the Call.

Later in 1923 I held meetings in Ottawa with Rev. A. W.

Roffe, assisted by the Coloured Male Quintet of Cleveland. Large crowds gathered and many were saved. Finally a great Tabernacle was erected under the leadership of Rev. E. B. Fitch. December found me in a glorious soul-saving campaign in St. Paul. Suddenly I was becoming widely known.

Thus from the year 1923 I was kept busy responding to calls from all over the United States and Canada, from Florida to California, a work that has never ceased from that day to this. For these openings I owe everything to The Christian and Missionary Alliance.

The year 1924 found me in Europe for the first time at the invitation of Pastor William Fetler, who opened up the great Russian mission fields to me, where I preached to vast congregations of Russians, Latvians and Poles. But that is a story in itself. Brief reports will be found in my books "The Passion for Souls" and "The Great Russian Revival". Pastor Fetler taught me much.

As for The Alliance Tabernacle, Christie Street, Toronto, it enjoyed a perennial revival. We lived, as it were, on the crest of a wave. Campaign after campaign was held, and souls saved continually. Miss Alice Porter left Dale Church and came to work with me, and together we laboured and toiled as the crowds thronged the huge auditorium, the largest work in the Alliance.

Thus the vision I received on the Pacific Coast was at least partially realized. My youthful dreams were coming true. My agonizing prayers had been answered. The Alliance Tabernacle, in a very real sense, had become "Toronto's Great Centre of Evangelism". So great were the crowds that twice it had to be enlarged. At times as many as 1,000 were turned away. Those who sat on the platform will never forget the inspiring sight as they gazed out over the vast sea of some 2,300 faces, far up to the top of the elevation and away off to the left in the Annex.

But best of all, God worked, and souls were saved. Scores upon scores crowded down the aisles and filled the Enquiry Rooms. Wonderful were the prayer meetings held and the answers received as God displayed His mighty power.

This was the beginning of evangelism in Toronto. It was something entirely new for a church to hold evangelistic meetings night after night, year out and year in, in a continuous soul-winning effort. Evangelistic songs were introduced, the invitation was given and souls were saved and set on fire to win others. At that time no other church even thought of doing it; we had the entire field to ourselves. But later our methods were copied by many others, though never to the same extent. God had given us the vision and the results were glorious.

There were many small churches and assemblies that specialized in Bible Teaching. Bible Teaching, we knew, was necessary, and so we set aside the Wednesday and Friday nights for Bible exposition. Then, too, we brought many outstanding Bible Teachers to our pulpit to hold Bible Conferences. But we knew that Bible Teaching in itself would not suffice. If the Church was to grow, hold its young people and reproduce, it must emphasize evangelism, for *the church that does not evangelize will fossilize*. There must be a well-balanced programme—Evangelism, Bible Teaching and Missions.

But—on June 20th, 1926, I preached my farewell sermon, and, with a heart rent and torn, turned away from my God-given task. The work that had become dearer than life itself, the child of my prayers and tears, born in the travail of my soul, was taken over by others. For a time the great crowds continued to attend, so solid had been the foundation upon which the work had been built. Never had there been the least sign of a split of any kind, for there were no difficulties. I had been manœuvred out when the work was at its very peak and all was well. The last missionary offering was $34,000.00, an amount never equalled since. Finally, people began to leave, the crowds disappeared and the enthusiasm waned, never to be revived. But perhaps it would be better for the present, at least, if I were to draw a veil over the Gethsemane of those months of torture and despair. I had lost all, or so it seemed, yet God had not forgotten me.

"I will bear the indignation of the Lord . . . until He plead my cause, and execute judgment for me; He will bring me forth to the light, and I shall behold His righteousness:" (Mic. 7: 9). This was God's Word to me, so I humbled myself and took courage.

I had been persuaded to resign by being offered the Superintendency of The Christian and Missionary Alliance for Eastern Canada, but little did I know that God had a plan for a much greater work in the years to come.

In all this glorious work in Toronto, from 1921 to 1926, without any thought of remuneration, Fred L. Syme, one of Eaton's managers, was our Soloist and Song Leader, and he hardly ever missed a service. May God richly reward him. He went to be with Christ on July 4, 1956. I never had a greater friend or helper.

LOS ANGELES

After campaigning throughout Ontario for some months, and then in Georgia, Florida and Texas, with much spiritual blessing and large crowds, I journeyed finally to California with my wife and three children, and their nurse, Chrissie French, having accepted a Call to the pastorate of The Gospel Tabernacle of the C. & M. A., Los Angeles, where I commenced work on April 10th, 1927. However, before I had been there a week, I knew I was not to stay. My heart was still in Toronto, and I was certain I would return, for my work in Toronto was not yet done. I decided to stay a year. Chrissie never forgot my prayer: "Lord, comfort our hearts."

I took over Trinity Auditorium seating 2,100 in the heart of Los Angeles. It was packed the first Sunday, May 29th, and a dozen or more were saved. Extra chairs had to be brought in the second Sunday to accommodate the crowd. Mr. S. E. Ramseyer built up a great choir and orchestra, and led them as only he could. He played the trombone and sang solos. His gifted wife was pianist and harpist. Sunday after Sunday for some six months, huge crowds attended and many were saved. R. G. Le Tourneau and his wife were members of my choir. Los Angeles has never forgotten Trinity Auditorium.

During my ministry The Gospel Tabernacle of Los Angeles was filled for the first time in its long history. So great were the crowds that chairs had to be placed in the aisles. I was succeeded as pastor by the famous Irish evangelist, Rev. Wm. P. Nicholson.

For three months with Rev. Michael Billester and Madam Marie Karinskaya, the famous Russian prima-donna, I campaigned for Russia, and we were able to send $10,000 to Pastor William Fetler for his Tabernacle in Riga, Latvia.

While praying one day in Los Angeles, God gave me this verse: "Oh that thou wouldest bless me indeed, and enlarge my coast" (1 Chron. 4: 10). How wonderfully that prayer has been answered! What a world-wide work was born. How marvellously He has enlarged my coast. Blessed be His name!

But—Toronto was calling, in my heart, and on April 1, 1928, I preached my farewell sermon in order to return to my own city to—nothing. Yet I had been offered every inducement to stay. Thousands had thronged my ministry, including Dr. W. E. Blackstone, not only in Los Angeles, but all over California, for with Mr. and Mrs. Ramseyer I travelled and campaigned far and wide and everywhere souls were saved. The people offered to build me a Tabernacle seating 3,000 if I would remain. They showered me with gifts from a watch and household furniture to a Nash car, but all to no avail, for my heart was in Toronto.

Leaving on May 16, 1928, with our three children and Chrissie, we motored the 3,000 miles home, over gravel roads and with serious tyre and engine trouble. Hope had the mumps most of the way. Never will we forget that trip. It took us twelve days to make it.

On June 3rd, 1928, at the invitation of the pastor, Rev. Ira David, I preached again in my own Tabernacle on Christie Street to a crowd that overflowed far into the Annex. Many responded to the invitation and walked down the aisles to accept Christ. But that was my last Sunday in the great Tabernacle of my toils and tears. Twenty-five years later it was sold to the Jews. As soon as I came back, I was made a member of the New York Board, and I expected to work with the Alliance the rest of my life.

After I returned, a weekly prayer meeting was held at the home of Mr. and Mrs. John A. Garrett, 686 Euclid Ave., to plead with God to again give me a work in Toronto. An average of a dozen of my former followers faithfully attended, and, on their faces before God, with many tears, agonized in prayer for another great soul-winning and missionary centre of evangelism. They were convinced that my work was not done and that God still wanted me in Toronto. Miss Porter led, but I was only able to be present a few times. These prayers were abundantly answered.

It was at this time in my life that the Holy Spirit came in His anointing power, first in Tampa, and then in Truro, as recorded in "The Enduement of Power." These were definite and glorious experiences.

CHAPTER IX

THE PEOPLES CHURCH

THE time had now come for the launching of my third and greatest work in the city of Toronto. The first had been Dale Presbyterian Church (1915), the second, The Alliance Tabernacle (1921), and now the third—The Peoples Church (1928). I was just 38 years of age.

I felt led to launch it in Massey Hall—Toronto's largest auditorium, then seating 3,400 people. I knew that if I started in a small building it would take years to get it going, but if I launched it in a large well known centre it would soon be on the map. So I chose Massey Hall.

Soon after our return from Los Angeles to Toronto I had resigned from the Christian and Missionary Alliance and joined Paul Rader, President of the Worldwide Christian Couriers, who appointed me Director for Canada and commissioned me to organize a soul-winning missionary work in Toronto, which I now did. Paul Rader and Clinton H. Churchill helped.

My first service was held on Sunday, September 9th, 1928. I called the new work The Cosmopolitan Tabernacle and held services every Sunday night in Massey Hall from September 9th to January 13th. Mr. W. C. Willis, my ever faithful friend, again became my treasurer. Miss Alice Porter was my secretary. Mr. H. H. Phinnemore, my head usher. Many souls were saved and tremendous spiritual blessing experienced.

Thus for over four months I had the privilege of preaching in the great Massey Hall, where D. L. Moody, R. A. Torrey, J. Wilbur Chapman, Gipsy Smith and many other world evangelists had held their campaigns and where I, when a boy of 16, had been converted. It was a thrilling experience and I will always be glad that Massey Hall became my church.

Mr. and Mrs. S. E. Ramseyer had charge of the music. Donald Billings was our pianist. At that first service, according to the newspapers, there were nearly 2,000 present and about a dozen came forward to accept Christ. The enthusiasm was tremendous.

Paul Rader, who was our President until I resigned from the Couriers in 1932, was a born leader. He was one of the greatest preachers of his generation. He could hold his audience spellbound for an hour and a half. He was a missionary promoter, evangelist and soul winner. He backed me in every way possible, young though I was, and I will always thank God for the privilege of having worked with him.

In 1929, Paul Rader asked me to visit the Russian mission fields of Europe and so, after preaching a farewell message in Massey Hall on January 13th, I left for my second trip abroad. When I returned in June, all my recommendations were accepted. A Bible school was established in Riga and missionaries sent to evangelize Latgalia. Work was undertaken among the refugees of France and Belgium. A Bible school was established in Spain and a dean sent out from the United States. Thus commenced our own great missionary work.

The first Courier Missionary Convention was held in Massey Hall when I returned, June 27 to 30, 1929, and we received an offering of $10,000. I then proceeded to the United States to raise money under the auspices of the Couriers for our European missionary work and God gave me in cash and faith promises some $60,000 during the following six months.

On Sunday, March 30, 1930, we moved to St. James Square Presbyterian Church, 42 Gerrard Street East, which Messrs. Day, Perkins and Ward had rented for evangelistic campaigns, calling it the Toronto Gospel Tabernacle. We took over their radio broadcast over CFRB, along with Eldon B. Lehman, their choir leader.

The Couriers' second Missionary Convention, which was held the first week, was closed by Paul Rader with an offering of $25,000 for Missions. The auditorium, which accommodated some 1,200, was packed to capacity with many standing.

For some time I did not take much interest in the work. My heart was not in it. I felt that it did not belong to me. My child was still on Christie Street, and I mourned for it as a father mourns for his son. Very often I left others in charge and travelled all over the United States holding campaigns.

On June 9th, 1932, I once more found myself in France on my third missionary tour, but that again is a story in itself.

On October 30th, 1932, when I was welcomed back, I was greeted by a full house with many standing, and from that day to this, except in the hot summer months, with but few exceptions, the crowds on Sunday nights have packed the auditorium to its utmost capacity.

At once I took heart again. My soul was revived. I forgot the child of my first love for I saw that my new work was destined to become greater and far more important than anything I had known before. It was a case of "the expulsive power of a new affection". God at last had healed my broken heart and had given me a work again. Yes, and the glory of this latter house, I had been assured, was to become greater, infinitely greater, than the former.

On October 1, 1933, I changed the name to *The Peoples Church*.

On July 1st, 1934, we moved to Central Methodist Church, 100 Bloor Street East, which had been left vacant by the Union. What a miracle of God's grace! I could hardly believe my good fortune. To think that God had given me such a large church, lovely cushioned pews, beautiful Italian architecture, and the most central location in the city, was almost too good to be true. It was a magnificent auditorium for evangelistic and missionary work, accommodating over 2,000 people. At long last my vision on the Pacific Coast was to be fulfilled and my dreams come true.

BUYING THE CHURCH

From time to time the people had urged me to buy or build a large church in Toronto, but I refused. My answer was always the same. I did not want to burden the congregation with a great debt, die and go to Heaven and leave the next pastor or generation to pay it off. Nor did I believe in making large interest payments to mortgage companies, that might be used for work in the Foreign Field. Hence I stood my ground.

"Not until someone gives me a cheque for at least $10,000," I said, "will I go ahead." That statement I made over the air again and again and every time I made it the people laughed. "The idea," they exclaimed, "of anyone giving $10,000 in one cheque."

"You have a large congregation," they argued. "Surely with 2,500 givers on the roll, you can buy a church. And look at your present auditorium; it is always crowded. Why wait?"

"No," I said, "not a move will I make till God gives me at least one large gift."

"But where is your faith?" they asked.

"The God Who can give the money after can just as easily give it before," I answered. "I have no right to incur debts and then expect God to come to my aid. If He wants me to go ahead, He will send the money FIRST. Then I will know it is His will."

And so I prayed, prayed month after month and year after year, until six years had passed while we paid rent.

On Nov. 16, 1936, I was invited to the home of a Christian business man and his wife, who had asked me to pray about his work. Mrs. Smith was with me, and the four of us had dinner together. Very frankly they asked us about our plans for the future and I told them that we could buy The Peoples Church for $65,000, but that I would want one-third in cash before making the purchase. Mrs. Smith could hardly believe her ears. If I had suggested $5,000, she thought, it would have been amazing enough. We had a most lovely evening, and after united prayer, took our departure. It was most touching to hear these two wealthy servants of God as they humbly prayed for wisdom and guidance.

The next morning they telephoned my wife and told her to tell me that they had decided to give $20,000 toward the purchase of the church. That was almost a third, and twice the amount I had assured the people I would some day get. Oh, how my heart leaped for joy! Never in my life had I received such a gift. Again and again I walked the floor, praising God for His amazing goodness. At last He had answered and had done the exceeding abundantly above. And what a time of rejoicing! Words fail to describe the interest and enthusiasm of the great congregation. As a matter-of-fact, the whole city was moved, until the buying of The Peoples Church became the general topic of conversation.

THE CROWDS COME

Mr. Lehman organized a great volunteer choir of 135 voices and an orchestra of forty pieces. For years we conducted a Back Home Hour Broadcast. Our entire evening service went out to multiplied thousands. For a time we were on the "air" for three hours each Sunday night. Years later, Walt Huntley built a radio studio in the church, and from 1953 to 1955 we broad-

cast over some 42 stations across Canada and throughout
the world, and it all came about through the illness of Redd
Harper.

We emphasized evangelism. Every Sunday I gave an invitation and from year to year approximately 300 to 500 decided
for Christ. Scores were saved in radioland. Even though we
stopped all newspaper advertising for several years, still we
could not accommodate the crowds.

We had a $40,000 pipe organ which took up the entire space
across the back above the gallery. Our people, seeing so many
being turned away Sunday after Sunday, began to pray, asking
God to send someone to buy the organ. Finally a Roman
Catholic priest came along and took a fancy to it. Now it is
in a Roman Catholic Church. We then built a second gallery
back of and above the first, and from the first Sunday it
was opened, it was filled and was ever after. Many have
come from the "elevation", as we call it, to accept Christ.
For a while we used pianos. Then we purchased a small pipe
organ and erected it back of the choir loft.

I once had a letter from the Fire Chief demanding that I cut
down my audiences. Policemen have walked in upon me just
before I have gone into the pulpit with the same request. Again
and again I have announced over the air: "The church is full,
stay home and listen in, there is no more room." Yet still
they came. Scores of times I have said, "Move to the left,"
in order to make more room.

Evangelism, I have proven, will pack any church. The converts generally remain and soon fill the pews. All through the
years evangelistic campaigns have been held, and most of the
world's greatest preachers have occupied the pulpit. In these
campaigns, souls have been saved and Christians edified and
built up in the Faith; while our personal workers have been
kept busy in the enquiry rooms.

Back in 1935 J. Edwin Orr, the world traveller, came to
The Peoples Church and held a campaign for two weeks, closing in Massey Hall with a packed auditorium. The world-
famous Gypsy Smith held two tremendous campaigns, and
again we had to take Massey Hall.

During our campaign in 1944 with "Jackie" Burris and his
eleven Musical Messengers, we moved from The Peoples
Church to Massey Hall, and from Massey Hall to Maple Leaf
Gardens, seating over 14,000, the only time it had ever been

engaged for such a purpose. On each of the two Sunday nights we had over 11,000 people present.

TRAVEL ABROAD

Year after year I have travelled from the Atlantic to the Pacific, and from the Gulf to Northern Canada, holding evangelistic campaigns and missionary conventions in the larger cities, but for every invitation I have accepted, a dozen have had to be refused.

In 1936 I received a cable inviting me to occupy the pulpit of Spurgeon's Tabernacle, London, for a few Sundays, and on June 14th I found myself preaching from that world-famed pulpit; and so commenced my fourth world tour, which again is a story in itself.

Then in 1938, in response to both cable and letters, and after consulting J. Edwin Orr, who gave me much helpful advice, I left for Australia, New Zealand and the Solomon Islands on my fifth world tour, where I experienced some of my greatest victories.

When I returned in November, after an absence of six and a half months, I showed my pictures each week to audiences that commenced coming at 5 o'clock in order to get a seat for the 8 o'clock service, so great was the interest. The church across the street was rented and, after speaking to more than 2,000 in The Peoples Church, I held a second service for those who had patiently waited in the other church.

During 1935 and 1940 I visited Cuba in the West Indies, and in 1941 Jamaica, where the Kingston meetings were held in the largest theatre. It was packed to suffocation for nine nights. Scores had to stand, hundreds were turned away and policemen had to get me through the crowds. In nine days over 800 came down the aisles and were dealt with by personal workers. It was a time of real spiritual blessing. Leaving Jamaica, I flew with my wife in the Clipper to Haiti, where I preached to throngs of hungry natives, including the President, and thence back to Miami.

During the summer of 1935 we conducted a conference in "The Highlands" where the entire church spent many happy hours. It is one of the loveliest spots in Muskoka, and perhaps we should have carried it on, but for several seasons it was discontinued. Mr. L. Watson was our manager.

For eight years, from 1936 to 1944, we conducted a Missionary Medical Institute at 14 Park Road, under the leadership of Miss Louise Kirby, where prospective missionaries were given a year's instruction in medicine and tropical diseases, which would have become a monumental work had it not been interrupted. Then on January 1st, 1943, we co-operated with the Russian Gospel Association in the launching of a Russian Bible Institute for the training of Russian students, 37 of whom went into active service.

Since 1921 we have published what is known as "The Peoples Magazine", and it has literally circled the globe.

Many of my closest associates have passed on. Mr. Malcolm left us some years ago; Mr. Watson followed and then Mr. Willis. The next to go home was Miss Porter, December 24th, 1942. Miss Porter had been with me for twenty-five years, rendering loyal and faithful service. Dr. E. Ralph Hooper, my dear co-labourer and prayer-partner, went home on June 13th, 1950. Fred Syme and Rev. Geo. W. Stenton died in 1956. Then Dr. P. W. Philpott, in 1957. Only God knows how much I miss them all.

Rev. P. W. Philpott, D.D., of Moody Church fame, became my Associate Pastor on July 1st, 1943, and was with me for nearly ten years. Rev. Paul B. Smith, B.A., my youngest son, became my Associate Pastor on September 1st, 1952. Rev. George W. Stenton was my Assistant Pastor from 1942 to 1956, when he went to be with the Lord. Rev. Robert Watt came to us as Assistant Pastor in 1954.

Our auditors are Gunn, Roberts & Co., chartered accountants. Numerous organizations with capable leaders co-operate in the work. Throughout the years the greatest of harmony has prevailed. Never have we had a split of any kind.

Fierce indeed have been the attacks of the enemy first from without and then from within. Satan's emissaries have ever been busy, but never yet have we answered or attempted to defend ourselves, so that all has redounded to the glory of God. The dogs bark, but the caravan moves on. The worse the accusations, the larger have been the contributions and the crowds. Some have given even because of the attacks. Thus God has vindicated at every step, for every knock has been a boost, and the work speaks for itself. My motto has been "No attack! No defence!"

ORGANIZATION

The Peoples Church is an independent work, standing pre-eminently for the conversion of souls, the edification of believers, and world-wide evangelism; emphasizing especially the four great essentials: Salvation, the Deeper Life, Foreign Missions, and our Lord's Return; endeavouring by every means to get the Message to the Christless masses, both at home and abroad, in the shortest possible time.

We believe in an unmutilated Bible; salvation through the blood of Christ; entire separation from the world; victory over all known sin through the indwelling Spirit; rugged consecration to sacrificial service; practical faith in the sufficiency of Christ for spiritual, temporal and physical needs; purifying hope of the Lord's return; and a burning missionary zeal for the bringing back of the King through world evangelization.

The Peoples Church has a Board of Managers to look after the business end of the work, a Board of Elders to take care of the spiritual work of the church, and a Board of Deacons to handle the loose plate offerings. A paid office staff is responsible for the envelopes. At present there are 13 managers, over 200 elders and 14 deacons, all men of missionary vision, and all teetotallers and non-smokers.

On February 21st, 1936, in order to avoid any possibility of private ownership or personal profit, we had the work incorporated under a Board of Directors, as a non-profit organization, and obtained a government charter. Our funds and property holdings therefore are thus completely safeguarded, for we can do only what our charter allows.

Those who have been born again and are interested enough to contribute regularly to our foreign missionary work, are considered adherents of the church. They do not join, but they are closer to us as they attend, give and serve, than they could possibly be had they been enrolled as members. If they have not given for three years they are automatically dropped, so that our list is always up-to-date. At the present time we have over 3,500 on our roll. We dedicate children, baptize believers, and observe the Lord's Supper, but we do not make baptism a door to communion and church membership.

The Peoples Church, I feel, has been the fulfilment of the vision on the log of July 11th, 1919, on the Pacific Coast. To God be the glory.

CHAPTER X

TOURING THE WORLD

NEARLY 2,000 years ago, the Lord Jesus Christ commanded His disciples to "Go into all the world and preach the Gospel". In obedience to that command the Apostle Paul left home and friends to set forth on a world tour that did not end until he had seen his Master face to face.

He might have lived quietly in Palestine. At least he need not have been idle; there was plenty to do. Thousands in his own country had never heard the Gospel. But Paul heard God's Call to the Regions Beyond, and he could not rest. A world vision was his. So, bidding farewell to Antioch, he set his face toward Europe. And because of that we are Christians. What if he had disobeyed? Where would America have been today?

I too, have felt the urge. It has come upon me again and again. Just when I get nicely settled, and look forward to years of home life with my family, suddenly I am arrested by the Spirit of God. I hear His Call, and I have to go. I am restless. My soul is stirred within me. A vision of earth's perishing multitudes grips my heart and sends me forth.

And that urge has taken me all over Canada and the United States. I was only eighteen when I found myself in British Columbia, preaching the Gospel to the Indians. Twelve times I have gone to Europe, as well as to Africa, Asia and Australia. And always with but one great, all-absorbing passion—to preach Christ. I would like to stay in Toronto with my family and my work, for the loneliness is almost unbearable, but I have learned from experience that I must obey God rather than man.

There's an urge upon my spirit that compels my feet to go,
And to those in heathen darkness I must God's salvation show;
As He called the great apostle, so He chooses men today;
I am one whom He has chosen and I dare not disobey.

Eighteen times it has been my privilege to tour the world, not including my visits to the West Indies, the Indians of Mexico and the Eskimos of Alaska. I have been in no less than 70 different countries. These tours were made in the years 1924, 1929, 1932, 1936, 1938, 1946, 1948, 1949, 1950, 1955, 1957, 1959 (two), 1960, 1961 (two), 1962, 1963 and full reports of each were published.

In 1924 I visited England, Holland, France, Switzerland, Germany, Lithuania, Latvia, Poland and Luxemburg.

In 1929 I visited England, France, Belgium, Monaco, Italy, Austria, Germany, Latvia, Esthonia, Lithuania, Spain, Poland, Switzerland and Belgium.

In 1932 I visited England, France, Spain, Egypt, Palestine, India, Ceylon, the Malay Peninsula, the Dutch East Indies, French Somaliland and Ethiopia.

In 1936 I visited England, France, Spain, Germany, Poland, Latvia, Sweden, Denmark, Czechoslovakia, Rumania, Bulgaria, Turkey, Greece, Yugoslavia, Hungary, Austria, Belgium and Scotland.

In 1938 I visited Hawaii, Samoa, Fiji, Australia, the Soloman Islands and New Zealand.

In 1946, with my wife, my youngest son and his wife, I spent five months campaigning in England, Ireland, Scotland, Wales and Eire.

In 1948 I visited Eire, England, Switzerland, Holland, Belgium, France, Italy, Germany and Iceland.

In 1949 I visited Scotland, Ireland, England and Iceland.

In 1950 I visited England, Belgium, Norway, Scotland, Germany and Denmark.

In 1955 my wife and I visited the Azores, Portugal, Senegal, Liberia, the Gold Coast, Congo, Northern Rhodesia, Southern Rhodesia, South Africa, the Anglo-Egyptian Sudan, Egypt, Italy, France, England, Scotland and Newfoundland.

In 1957 my wife and I toured Brazil, Argentina, Chile, Peru, Equador, Colombia, Panama, and held eight great campaigns. For the first time in history all the churches co-operated and crowds of 25,000 attended. There were 4,500 first-time decisions for Christ. They were the largest united evangelistic campaigns in the history of South America. Mrs. E. Spitzer arranged them.

In the Spring of 1959 Mrs. Smith and I toured Iceland, Norway, Sweden, Finland, England, Ireland, Eire and Scotland, speaking to large gatherings on salvation, missions and the deeper life. It was during this tour that we were received in Buckingham Palace.

During the Fall of the same year we held meetings in various parts of Japan at the invitation of the Committee for the Centenary of Missions, and then conducted a campaign in Hong Kong, preaching to some 3,000 a night, followed by a Missionary Conference in Honolulu.

In 1960 I visited Alaska and Japan and held the largest united city-wide campaign ever to be held in the Kyoritz Hall, Tokyo. It seats 2,200 and it was packed out. Better still, there were nearly 1,000 decisions for salvation.

In 1961 Mrs. Smith and I visited Hawaii, Fiji and Australia. We preached to overflow crowds everywhere and met many of the converts of 23 years ago. Over 1,000 young people volunteered for foreign service and we were given $11,000 for Missions.

During the same year we toured England, Germany, Italy, Kenya, Rhodesia, South Africa, Sudan, and reached thousands.

In 1962 I held a campaign in Reykjavik, Iceland.

In 1963, with my wife, Chrissie French, and Jimmie McDonald, I held nation-wide campaigns in Ireland; I also went to England and Wales.

I am not going to write of them here, for each tour is a story in itself. Perhaps some day a more adequate lifestory will be written and the thrilling and dangerous experiences that I encountered in my world-wide travels in distant places where death lurked far too often, and trials and tribulations beset me as I followed new trails through great Russian forests and to pioneer outposts, will all be told. They were published at the time in *The Peoples Magazine, The Courier* and *The Defender*.

Suffice it to say that I experienced, on many a foreign field, something of the revival that Charles G. Finney knew. Huge crowds gathered and men and women in hundreds, weeping over their sins, thronged the aisles and the enquiry rooms and were gloriously saved. Especially was this true on the Russian fields. In Australia, New Zealand and South Africa it was difficult to find buildings large enough to take care of the crowds. In South Africa nearly 7,000 white people made decisions of one kind and another for Christ. In South America, nearly 10,000. To God be all the glory.

My greatest trials came from loneliness and illness. Only

D

those who have been far from home for months at a time in foreign lands know what it is to be lonely. As for sickness, I was very ill and weak in Spain. For six weeks I was desperately ill in Africa, much of the time in bed; while in the Solomon Islands and Australia I was almost at death's door with malaria fever, from which I suffered many severe attacks for three years after my return. Only those who have experienced the awful chills, the burning fever and the utter exhaustion of malaria, know the indescribable suffering endured. But God brought me through.

OUR MISSIONARY WORK

We started by contributing a small amount of a few thousand dollars each year, and then, year by year, as the interest grew, we increased our givings, until in 1961 we received over $300,000 for missions.

Away back in 1929 I organized what is now known as The Peoples Missionary Society, and at first we supported only some fifty or sixty Russian and Spanish nationals in Europe. Finally we were contributing toward the personal support of 360 missionaries, in 40 different countries, under 35 Faith Missions, at a cost of over $300,000 a year.

In 1929 we established a Bible School in Latvia, and later another in Spain. Fifty of our graduates were then sent all over Latgalia as well as Spain, evangelizing. Drunkards and wife-beaters were wonderfully saved. Thousands heard the Gospel, and some 3,000 were converted. I will ever thank God for the glorious work in Latgalia and Spain. By using a room on the third floor of 22 Kendal Avenue for an office, so as to avoid expense, I was able to send thousands of dollars to Europe for the support of the workers.

About the same time we turned to French Indo-China and the Dutch East Indies where we supported forty-three national evangelists under the C. & M. A., who reached thousands among the unevangelized tribes of these vast territories.

Our most fruitful field has been the West Indies, where the work is carried on by the Unevangelized Fields Mission, and the West Indies Mission. Bible Schools have been built on the different islands, and already over 80,000 have been saved.

It was in 1934 we turned to the Faith Missionary Societies in an effort to reach the whole world with the Gospel, and now for years past we have been pouring hundreds of thousands of dollars into the work. It is a glorious story, but it cannot be written here. Our magazine contains the reports, and my book, "The Cry of the World," reveals the secret.

The work of The Peoples Missionary Society is to stimulate missionary interest and raise funds wherever possible for the support of missionaries and missionary work throughout the world. It does not employ missionaries of its own. Those it supports serve with a number of well accredited Faith Missions working in pioneer fields. I discovered that many splendid missionaries did not receive regular and full allowances, and I determined to do what I could to relieve them of financial anxiety that they might do their best work. A new society, I felt, was not necessary.

Then, too, I realized the importance of our Lord's injunction when He told us to pray that labourers might be thrust out. The trouble was, He pointed out, a plenteous harvest but few labourers. Hence, I began asking God to burden the various Societies to send out more missionaries, and to encourage them to do so, we offered the personal support, if needed, of all who might go from Canada. Thus began a new day and a great advance for a number of the Faith Missions.

Our policy at the beginning was to take care of the full "personal" support that the missionary actually received as an allowance upon which to live. Faith Missions base their allowance on "needs", not "worth". We always send out the full amount received for missionary support. Nothing is deducted for administration. The Church takes care of the overhead.

We have worked with the Faith Missions because they are absolutely free of modernism and higher criticism. They are true to the Word of God. Their vision is to evangelize the unreached millions of earth and bring back the King. They do not major on institutional, educational and medical work. Their reliance is on God rather than on the church, and they practise self-denial and sacrifice.

But before long we had more money than workers, and it is interesting to recall the difficulty we had in investing our funds. Of course, it would have been easy to have given cheques to various Societies and let them do what they liked, but that was not our policy. God had given us another vision. We desired to see new workers going forth and we wanted to definitely and regularly support them.

So, in 1934, through the co-operation of Dr. Robert H. Glover, Home Director of the China Inland Mission, we invited a number of Faith Missions to our Convention and commenced by sending out and supporting missionaries under them. This resulted in a large number of new recruits, and was the beginning of united missionary conventions.

During these past years we have seen over 6½ million dollars raised for Missions in our Toronto work alone, and, in addition, as much more for other churches.

The amounts actually received for Missions, year by year, in The Peoples Church have been as follows:—$14,750, $43,891, $36,660, $36,151, $23,586, $27,181, $28,102, $36,290, $30,615, $40,029, $39,083, $46,435, $54,417, $60,279, $78,413, $117,723, $114,854, $122,440, $138,394, $177,473, $180,878, $177,076, $216,443, $228,960, $245,260, $280,423, $253,405, $289,502, $298,316, $282,221, $303,345, $329,240.

The total at the end of 1967 for all purposes was $8,921,399. Of this amount $6,555,824 was given for Missions.

Our plan has been to hold a great annual Missionary Convention featuring the so-called Faith Missions, with sessions both afternoon and evening each day for four weeks. Missionaries from all over the world are invited. Pictures are shown and addresses given. New recruits testify and tell why they are going to the field. Exhibits of curios and missionary literature are displayed. Thus a missionary vision is imparted, and the people come to know that "The Supreme Task of the Church is the Evangelization of the World".

Eager crowds attend, and hours are spent between sessions in the exhibit room, where refreshments are served; and then on each Sunday of the Convention, the annual missionary offering in faith-promises, amid great rejoicing, is received. We do not take up pledges; we use faith-promises.

From time to time our young people leave for the field. There is always a solemn service of dedication just before they go, when the Elders lay hands upon them and set them apart for the work to which God has called them.

We teach our people that missions come first. Everything else is secondary. "The Gospel must *first be* published among all nations" (Mark 13: 10). And when we seek first the extension of God's Kingdom, world wide, all other things needful are added.

Our people do not give as the world gives, namely, out of sympathy. We have taught them to give in order to carry out God's programme, which is to evangelize the unevangelized tribes of earth and thus bring back the King. (Rev. 5: 9, 7: 9. Acts 1: 8. Mark 13: 10. Matt. 24: 14.) Our policy is:

"To hasten the return of our Lord by following His programme for this age, which is to 'preach the gospel in all the world for a witness to all nations,' and, 'to take out of them a people for His name'. Our aim is to work among peoples, tribes and nations where Christ is not named."

We see to it that we give more to missions than we spend on ourselves, and there never has been a year since I have been Pastor of The Peoples Church when we have kept as much for ourselves for our current expenses as we have given for missions. For instance, in 1962 we spent $53,000 on ourselves, and over $318,000 for missions, more than six times as much. For many years our missionary obligation was so heavy that we felt we could not afford a paid assistant pastor. More than 76% of our total income has gone to missions—well over 6½ million dollars.

Many churches use what they need for themselves first, and then if there is anything left over they give it to missions. We have reversed the order, and have set aside a certain definite sum for missions each year, and then if anything is left over, we spend it on ourselves. In other words "first things first" has been our motto, for "The Mission of the Church is Missions". Long ago The Peoples Church voted me a salary of $6,000.00 a year, in addition to a car and other extras, but I have refused to accept more than $5,000.00. Moreover, all profits on my books—tens of thousands of copies—belong to the church. On January 1st, 1963, at my request, my salary was reduced to $3,000 a year.

We bought and paid for The Peoples Church in five years at a cost of $75,000, a property that may be worth a million dollars. But the point is, we increased our missionary givings, even when we were buying the church. We kept the same old carpet on the floor, and the same old cushions on the pews, for years, and we left the walls unpainted rather than let our missionary givings suffer. The reason many a church has nothing to give to missions is because it needs all its money for mortgage and interest payments. God says "Owe no man anything". Why then should a church owe money?

Scores of other churches have caught the vision. I held an evangelistic campaign in the famous Park Street Congregational Church, Boston, of which the Rev. Harold J. Ockenga, Ph.D., is the pastor, and the next year I was invited to hold a missionary convention, the first for that church in 135 years. They had only been giving $3,200 a year to missions. Each year for six years I went back. Today they are giving over $275,000 a year. The same is true of Grace Chapel, Philadelphia. When I held the first convention they were giving less than $10,000.00. Today they are contributing more than $100,000.00 a year to Missions. I held their convention each year for five years.

A ROMAN CATHOLIC REACTION

The following article from a Roman Catholic publication is well worth preserving, so I am quoting it here. It happened in 1937.

"No doubt many of our readers noticed with interest, a short time ago, the account in a Toronto paper of the annual 'foreign mission' collection taken up in The Peoples Church, Toronto. The total offering was the staggering sum of $43,272.00. We have no hesitation in saying that many Catholics must have noted the figures—blinked several times—and then turned to the next page with a remark to the effect that The Peoples Church must be attended exclusively by millionaires.

"At first, we confess, we found it difficult to believe—that one Protestant church in Toronto would give more than all the Catholic churches in Ontario and Western Canada—but there it was in cold type, upbraiding us for our lukewarmness and indifference in spreading the knowledge of Christ among the pagan people of the world.

"Of course, if all parishioners of The Peoples Church were millionaires—but the brutal fact—as we knew full well—was that they were nothing of the kind. They were just plain Protestant people—whose enthusiasm for foreign missions had been fired by a zealous pastor. To this latter, Rev. Oswald J. Smith, D.D., we addressed a note asking for certain information. Dr. Smith's kind and prompt reply really startled us— and dissipated our one possible explanation, viz., that a very few wealthy people had contributed the major portion of this record sum. Should not we as Catholics hang our heads in the face of such a withering contrast from our Protestant friends?

"We rejoice in the possession of the true Faith. We believe that Christ commanded US to see to it that His Gospel was preached 'to every people',—yet what do we find? One Protestant church in Toronto gives more money to the foreign mission cause than ALL the Catholic churches from Ottawa to Victoria. The lesson is there—writ so plainly that even he who runs may read—that we must catch some of our Protestant neighbours' enthusiasm. We—the custodians of Christ's Gospel —are sitting idly by while others gather in the harvest which the Master definitely ordered us to reap. Shall we continue? Please God it shall not be." Thus our achievements were being used to shame Catholics into giving.

WORKING WITH GOD

At one time Baptista Films made a sound film of me preaching one of my missionary messages, and called it "Go Ye". In 1952 they made another, "The Passion for Souls", which presents a real challenge, and is for rent or sale.

The greatest passion of my early life was to be a revivalist, to hold great evangelistic campaigns and see whole cities moved for God. For awhile I was the evangelist for the Cleveland Coloured Quintette, in fact, I started them out on their ministry. Had I continued with them, I could have toured the world in evangelism and preached to enormous crowds.

But it seemed as though God wanted me to have a head-quarters for my evangelistic campaigns, and to build a work for Him in Toronto, a work that would reach out to the whole world through a missionary programme of which I had never even thought. Hence the original vision had to take a secondary place, for never in my wildest imaginations did I dream of becoming known as a "missionary statesman" or of being advertised as "the pastor of the world's greatest missionary church", or of being announced as having raised more money for missions "than any living man". All this came to me unsought. I simply endeavoured to do the job to which God had called me and He did the rest.

CHAPTER XI

CONVENTION EXPERIENCES

IT MAY be of interest to quote some of the reports of past years to show the spirit of the Missionary Conventions held in The Peoples Church and the enthusiasm of the people.

1934

"Our Annual Missionary Convention has closed. The total offering was $29,000, namely $4,000 above our objective, and $7,000 over last year. God be praised!

"Words are inadequate to express the spirit and enthusiasm of the last day. At the close of the afternoon service only about one-half the objective had been received. Then came the evening service, and oh, what an experience! Never will we forget it. Multiplied thousands are praising God today for what He did.

"The auditorium of The Peoples Church was not only filled to capacity, but more than 200 were compelled to stand around the walls after every available seat had been taken and a large number had been turned away. And this great audience stayed right with us until the benediction was pronounced.

"As the offering increased the enthusiasm of the people rose until from every side men and women were praising God and eagerly waiting for each announcement. Chorus after chorus was sung, led by the choir and orchestra under the direction of Eldon B. Lehman.

"A special telephone had been installed near the pulpit, and as the pastor, Dr. Oswald J. Smith, announced the number over the air, the bell continued to ring throughout the entire service. Radio listeners from near and far phoned in their gifts, some from out of town. Soon a second phone had to be utilized, and even then it was next to impossible to take all the calls. Interest increased and enthusiasm rose to fever heat as amount after amount was announced from the pulpit.

"During the whole of the Back Home Hour the telephone rang and gifts were registered every few minutes. So great was the interest that nearly $4,000 came in by telephone alone. Extra time was secured on the Air, so that the service did not close until 11.15 p.m., and still the people stayed.

"Dr. Smith called for volunteers, and approximately 150 young people stood to their feet, signifying their willingness to give their lives for foreign service.

"Finally the grand total was announced, $29,000, and to say that the vast audience was electrified is putting it mildly. Never in the history of The Peoples Church has such an offering been received, and that in a time of financial depression. Again we say, Glory to God in the highest!"

1937

"Another great Annual Missionary Convention has closed. The offering laid at the Master's feet on Sunday, April 18th, was over $43,000, while 240 young people volunteered for foreign service. Praise the Lord!

"Five great services were held on the closing day. The first was at 11 a.m., when the auditorium was filled. The second was at 3 in the afternoon. The third service was scheduled to commence at 7, but on account of the great crowd filling the enlarged auditorium to its utmost capacity, with scores standing, it started away before the hour and continued until 8.30, the entire programme being broadcast. The fourth service started at 9.30 and continued until 10.30, the auditorium being filled to the top seat in the second gallery. It, too, was broadcast. The closing service of the day commenced at 11 o'clock at night, when the grand total of over $43,000 was announced, after which the choir and orchestra sang and played the 'Hallelujah Chorus', Eldon B. Lehman leading."

1939

"Fifty thousand dollars! Such was the amount announced on Sunday, April 30th, the closing day of the Annual Missionary Convention.

"To describe the interest, enthusiasm and excitement would be impossible. It increased as the hours passed by, until, at night, people were sitting in the aisles, on the floor, and standing up around the walls on every side.

"The last service commenced at 9.30 p.m. and closed at 10.30, and the crowd was larger than ever. Everyone waited to hear the verdict, which came about three minutes before going off the air. There was a breathless interest as Dr. Smith finally made the announcement. At first the people cheered and applauded. Hundreds of exclamations of praise to God ascended from all parts of the vast audience, and then the Doxology was sung as it has seldom been sung even in The Peoples Church."

1944

"The largest missionary offering ever received in The Peoples Church and, so far as we know, in the whole of Canada, was announced by Dr. Oswald J. Smith on Sunday night, April 30th, to a congregation that packed the church to its utmost capacity.

"The offering last year was $77,000. The amount that actually came in was over $78,000. But this year broke all records, the offering being over $106,000.

"It would be impossible to describe the enthusiasm of the people. The great auditorium was filled again and again throughout the day, scores upon scores being compelled to stand. Choruses were sung and many an 'Amen' and 'Praise the Lord' was heard as Dr. Smith called out the amounts. Rev. Peter Deyneka assisted. His enthusiasm was contagious. Again and again the people broke out in applause. There were many tear-stained eyes as the offering mounted higher and higher.

"When the offering got up to approximately $90,000 and the people were so excited that they could hardly contain themselves, suddenly Dr. Harold Strathearn was called upon by Dr. Smith to say a word, and no one who was present will ever forget what he said.

"Dr. Smith thought he was going to make an announcement about Mr. LeTourneau's magazine, but instead he told the people that Mr. LeTourneau had decided, after having been present at the morning service, to make a donation of $10,000 to the missionary fund. To describe the scene that followed his announcement, would be impossible. The great congregation rose and sang the Doxology. It was so unexpected that the enthusiasm of those present knew no bounds."

1949

"It was ten-thirty Sunday night. The Peoples Church was packed for its fourth service of the day. All around the sides people were standing, unable to get seats, and they had been standing since 6.45 p.m., over three and a half hours. Away up in the elevation the aisles were crowded, while numbers stood everywhere in the gallery. The triumphant strains of the Hallelujah Chorus had just died away and the atmosphere was electric.

"A few minutes earlier the pastor, Dr. Oswald J. Smith, amid breathless silence, had announced the grand total—$181,000. It was a momentous occasion. Thousands had prayed and God had sent in the largest offering ever given in the history of The Peoples Church. The present missionaries—over 200, could now be supported for another year, and thirty-eight new ones, already accepted, sent out."

1951

"An immense crowd thronged every inch of space. Enthusiasm was running high. It was the fourth service of the day. Some 9,000 people had attended. Hundreds were standing. As Dr. Smith mounted the platform the audience awaited in breathless silence the announcement of the grand total—$225,000.00. A crescendo of joyful praise gripped the vast assembly, as the people united with the splendid choir in singing the Hallelujah Chorus.

"Over 50,000 had attended during the three weeks of the Convention. This was the first time in history that a missionary convention had been held for such a long period. There had been no begging for funds. No solicitors had ever been sent from door to door. It was God's people getting God's vision and carrying out God's programme. It was giving to evangelize the world and bring back the King. It was a red-letter day in my experience." Dr. Fred D. Jarvis of Japan.

1952

The objective this year was a quarter of a million dollars. The amount received was $258,000.00. It was the longest convention in the world's history—three weeks, four Sundays and one day. A total of 54,000 people attended—8,000 each Sunday. The Peoples Church now has over 300 missionaries. Never in our wildest imaginations did we ever expect to see a quarter of a million dollars raised for missions. "This is the Lord's doing, and it is marvellous in our eyes."

1954

The Convention lasted for four weeks and five Sundays. It was the longest ever held. There were three meetings each day and four on Sundays. On the last Sunday there were more than 8,000 at the four services. Hundreds had to stand and many were turned away. Rev. Paul B. Smith assisted in the Convention.

As soon as the Thermometer was broken the Choir sang the Hallelujah Chorus. For the first time the afternoon service saw the total reach a quarter-of-a-million dollars and, for the first time, the Thermometer was broken during the 7 o'clock service. On Saturday 250 people met for an emergency prayer meeting. The objective was $265,000.00, but God answered and sent in $270,000.00.

1955

To describe the scene at 10.30 p.m., when Dr. Smith announced the grand total of $290,000.00 would be impossible. It was $25,000.00 above the goal. The service started at 6.25 p.m., so great was the crowd, and the people stood until 10.30 —452 by actual count—after nearly 2,000 had been seated. It was the largest offering for Missions ever received.

The next ten years, however, it was over $300,000.00 each year. Dr. Paul B. Smith conducted it in 1960 when his father was ill and the offering was $314,000.00. In 1962 it was $325,000.00. The total amount for Missions is now (1966) over six million dollars.

CHAPTER XII

THE STORY OF MY HYMNS

NEVER will I forget the thrill that was mine when I saw the first printed copies of two of my hymns. It was in 1914 when I was twenty-four. The music was by Dr. D. B. Towner, and he it was who sent them to me. My whole being was electrified as I gazed at them. The ecstasy of that moment will never be erased. I was then in South Chicago.

But in those early years only a few of my hymns ever really saw the light of day. I wrote scores, but for years it was a struggle with many discouraging experiences. True, my hymn poems were accepted by various composers, but for some reason they were seldom used.

I have never written in a mechanical way just for the sake of writing. As a rule I wait until I am passing through some great crisis, and then I cannot help writing. And because they have been born out of personal experiences, they appeal to others.

Those who study them will get a glimpse into the spiritual struggles and mental experiences through which I have passed. They sound the deepest depths and the highest heights of my inner life, for they have been my greatest source of comfort and relief.

When writing them I have been drawn unusually close to God. Moments of ecstasy and exaltation of spirit indescribable have been mine. For in my hours of deepest depression and heartache I have found an outlet for my feelings and emotions in writing poetry.

HOW I STARTED

My early work was with Dr. D. B. Towner, of the Moody Bible Institute, and after his death, George C. Stebbins of D. L. Moody fame. Both of these men wrote music for many of my hymns and Charles M. Alexander published them. Dr. Towner gave wings to my hymns "Jesus Only" and "Christ is

Coming Back Again." The latter has now become a great choir number. He wrote for and published several others.

Dr. Towner and Chas. M. Alexander died, and after that for years I did little or nothing, and it looked as though my hymn writing was at an end. I had written a couple hundred or more, among them some that are now world famous.

Then, one day, in the Churchill Tabernacle, Buffalo, in 1930, when I was 40, I met the world's greatest living composer of gospel music, B. D. Ackley. Again I began to write. Hymn after hymn I sent to him, and the music that he wrote so fitted the words that they were in immediate demand. They were brought out by The Rodeheaver Co., and they have now published more than 200 of my hymns and gospel songs, among them the following favourites:

In 1931—Joy in Serving Jesus.
In 1932—Only Jesus Satisfies—Satisfied with Thee—The Saviour Can Solve Every Problem.
In 1933—A Revival Hymn—Have I Grieved Thy Holy Spirit?
In 1934—The Glory of His Presence—Happy Days Will Come Again—Let Me Forget.
In 1935—Take Thou, O Lord—Where Dreams Come True.
In 1936—After—His Love is All My Plea—The Breaking of the Day—Do Not Worry.
In 1937—When the Autumn Leaves Have Turned to Gold —God Understands—Let King Jesus Reign.
In 1938—God is in the Shadows—The Dawning of the Morning—God is Waiting in the Silence—Pray On—The Song of the Soul Set Free.
In 1939—The Broken Threads of Life—The Need of the World is Jesus—Waiting on Jesus.
In 1940—Then Jesus Came—With Thy Spirit Fill Me.
In 1941—A Wedding Prayer.
In 1942—Surrender.
In 1944—Be Thou Near—He Rose Triumphantly.
In 1945—Beyond the Shadows—I will Trust.
In 1946—The Finest of the Wheat—The Hour that Refreshes.
In 1949—The Bitter and the Sweet—Forgive Me for Forgetting—My Heart's Desire.

In 1950—The Man of Galilee—Never Forgotten—When Day is Done.

In 1956—A Song in My Soul.

In 1957—Jesus Met Me.

In 1958—The Saviour's Touch—I hear My Saviour's Voice—His Way is Best.

In 1959—Onward with Christ.

In 1961—A Crown of Glory.

In 1967—Jesus Lives Today.

Almost immediately America's leading soloists began singing them both on the air and to audiences all over the country. It was not long before "Then Jesus Came", "The Glory of His Presence", "God Understands", "Satisfied with Thee", "Where Dreams Come True", "The Saviour Can Solve Every Problem", "Let King Jesus Reign", "With Thy Spirit Fill Me", "He Rose Triumphantly", "The Song of the Soul Set Free", etc., were known throughout the world. These hymns have now been collected and put into a 64-page book and published by The Rodeheaver Company—"Oswald Smith's Best Songs". Many have been recorded. Capitol Records has made a wonderful album of my songs for the Christian Faith Recording Co. Diadem has made another.

One of the greatest surprises of my life was to get into the cowboy world. I had been preaching to a group of movie and entertainment people in Hollywood, and, as a result, Redd Harper (Mr. Texas) wrote western music to several of my lyrics. They were published in sheet music and recorded. They include, among others, "I'm Singing for My Lord", "Come With Your Heartache," and "The End of Life's Journey." It was in one of my meetings in the home of Stuart Hamblin that Lee Childs, the Shakespearean actress, was saved. She too wrote for me. Cindy Walker and Tim Spencer had introduced me.

Finally I sold 210 of my hymns to the Zondervan Music Co. and put the money into missions. They have now published a book of them called "Oswald J. Smith's Favourites".

HOW I WROTE THEM

The stories of these hymns make interesting reading. Here are some of my recollections of them:

"DEEPER AND DEEPER"

On August 13, 1911, when I was twenty-one years of age, I preached in Central Methodist Church, the largest in Woodstock, Ontario. As I walked along the street that Sunday morning the melody of this hymn sang itself into my heart, and with it the words, "Into the heart of Jesus, deeper and deeper I go." I wondered if I could retain the music in my mind until after the service. I did, and as soon as I got back to my room I wrote it out, and it has never been changed from that day to this.

The verses were quite difficult. It was three years later, at the age of twenty-four, in the First Presbyterian Church of South Chicago, of which I was pastor (1914), that they were completed. The writing of them afforded me much joy. Since then the hymn has appeared in a number of books and has been a great comfort. The large Baptist Church Choir, Dallas, has recorded it.

"ALONE WITH THEE"

My favourite hymn is "Alone With Thee". I dictated the words as they came to me to Myrtle Donahue, who wrote them down, when I was twenty-four years of age, at Winona Lake, Indiana, August 30th, 1914. They were born of a deep heart experience. The music I wrote in Toronto when I was twenty-five. Many a lonely heart has found comfort in this hymn.

Alone, dear Lord, ah, yes! alone with Thee!
My aching heart at rest, my spirit free;
My sorrow gone, my burdens all forgotten,
When far away I soar alone with Thee.

"A REVIVAL HYMN"

I wrote "A Revival Hymn", both words and music, in the year 1916, when I was 26, during an awakening in Dale Church, Toronto. But it was not until Mr. Ackley gave the words a new setting seventeen years later that it became popular.

"SAVED"

One of my best known hymns is "Saved", owned and published by the Hope Publishing Co. It was born in Toronto in the year 1917, when I was twenty-seven. The music was written by Roger M. Hickman. Arthur W. McKee was the first to introduce it. To hear the great Massey Hall audience sing this hymn during the Paul Rader campaign was an experience never to be forgotten. It is known and sung throughout America. It was the first to achieve popularity.

THE GLORY OF HIS PRESENCE

"The Glory of His Presence" was published in 1934. It expresses failure, disappointment and restoration, and it was written out of a deep heart experience. Today it is perhaps the favourite solo of all I have written. The music is by B. D. Ackley.

Rev. A. H. Ackley, D.D., wrote: "I am still humming 'The Glory of His Presence.' No lovelier Gospel song has appeared in twenty years than this gem. It probes the depths of my being with emotion and holy desire every time I sing it or hear it."

Later, he wrote this: " 'The Glory of His Presence' still rings down the corridors of my being. It abides the winnowing process of time as one of the very greatest of hymns—sweet, thrilling, glorious."

Then he wrote: "I have been hearing your lovely lyric 'The Glory of His Presence' quite frequently lately on the Radio. You know what I think of this beautiful number. It stands out like a giant Andes among the many beautiful Gospel lyrics you have written. This song—in my humble opinion—has the lasting quality that includes it among the classics. It is a song that never 'runs dry.' It brings inspiration to all who hear it. I have seen it move men Christ-ward many, many times. I might call it a 'fish-hook' song. It gets into the heart with its barb of sweetness and one cannot get it out. That, to me, is a real test of a great song."

In 1958 he wrote this: "I still believe that the very finest, if not the loveliest, song you have ever written is 'The Glory of His Presence.' If ever a song was inspired by the Spirit of God, this song was. It seems to have everything that makes for a thrilling, uplifting, soul-moving song. Very few approach it— none, in my opinion, excels it. It's a truly great song."

I have walked alone with Jesus
In a fellowship divine;
Never more can earth allure me,
I am His and He is mine.

In the darkness, in the shadow,
With the Saviour I have trod,
Sweet indeed have been the lessons,
Since I've walked alone with God.

"GOD UNDERSTANDS"

My youngest sister and her husband, Rev. and Mrs. Clifford Bicker, were preparing for their first furlough. Two little children had been born in Peru. Shortly before the boat sailed Clifford was instantly killed in an automobile accident, and my little sister, leaving her husband's body in South America, came home with her two fatherless children, a widow at twenty-six. To her I dedicated "God Understands," and she got it before leaving the field. It was a comfort to Ruth ; it has been a comfort to thousands of others. That was in 1935. B. D. Ackley wrote the music.

God understands your sorrow,
  He sees the falling tear,
And whispers, "I am with thee,"
  Then falter not, nor fear.

God understands your heart-ache,
  He knows the bitter pain ;
Oh, trust Him in the darkness,
  You cannot trust in vain.

"LET KING JESUS REIGN"

I was preaching in Pastor Findlay's Tabernacle, Glasgow, Scotland, September, 1936. One night John Geddes spoke. During his address he told this story : "When the armies of the Covenanters met for worship in the hills and dales of Scotland, before going into battle, they raised the right arm and cried : 'Let King Jesus Reign'." Immediately my attention was arrested, and getting out my pad I began to write. By the time he had finished his address I had written most of the hymn, "Let King Jesus Reign". Bringing it back to America, I sent it to Mr. Ackley, who wrote the inspiring tune to which it is now sung by choirs and quartettes.

"THE SONG OF THE SOUL SET FREE"

This is the song that Billy Graham is featuring in his great campaigns. It has become a most popular tenor and soprano solo, and choir number. Rev. A. H. Ackley sent me the beautiful musical setting to which I quickly wrote the words and it was published in 1938. I love its message, and so does everyone else.

"THE NEED OF THE WORLD IS JESUS"

One afternoon, in the year 1939, I received a letter from Mr. Ackley enclosing a music manuscript. He was anxious, so he stated, to get it into the new book now ready for the press. But it had no words. I went to work immediately, and by midnight had the words ready. They were mailed the next morning. Mr. Ackley rushed them to Chicago. A plate was made, and the beautiful congregational number, "The Need of the World is Jesus" appeared in the new book, Christian Service Songs.

"THEN JESUS CAME"

I was standing by Mr. Ackley's piano in Philadelphia when Homer Rodeheaver walked in. "I want a hymn," he said, "depicting the change that took place in the lives of men when Jesus came." And he went on at length, describing what he had in mind. I made a mental note of his request, and next day, May 1939, I had the poem, "Then Jesus Came," ready. Dr. Rodeheaver wrote most appropriate music to it, and for years he sang it. As Mr. Ackley played it over, Dr. Rodeheaver graphically portrayed the different scenes as he sang the song. It has become a great favourite and is sung everywhere. It has often been sung by Bev. Shea on Billy Graham's Hour of Decision programme. He recorded it.

When Jesus comes, the tempter's power is broken,
When Jesus comes, the tears are wiped away;
He takes the gloom and fills the life with Glory,
For all is changed when Jesus comes to stay.

"A WEDDING PRAYER"

I wrote "A Wedding Prayer" for my daughter, Hope, a few days before I married her to Donovan Lowry, and read it during the ceremony. Later it was published in The Peoples Magazine. Rev. A. H. Ackley, the noted composer, saw it and was immediately gripped by the words. He at once wrote the beautiful music to which it is now sung. Hope was married on August 17th, 1940, and since then it has been heard at hundreds of weddings all over the world.

"BEYOND THE SHADOWS"

In the year 1943, when I was holding meetings in Calgary, Rev. and Mrs. N. W. Enfield invited me to have dinner with them. On the way Mrs. Enfield informed me that her husband had only six months to live. It made a deep impression on me, and, as I ate with him that day, I could not help but think of the tragedy that awaited him.

While travelling by train on October 2nd, I wrote "Beyond the Shadows" for him, and sure enough, six months later he was with the Lord. B. D. Ackley wrote the touching music to which it is now sung, and immediately it became a favourite.

Beyond the shadows the dawn is breaking,
The night of darkness will soon be o'er;
My Saviour calls me, the day is waking,
And soon I'll see Him Whom I adore.

"HE ROSE TRIUMPHANTLY"

Malaria fever is not always conducive to hymn-writing, but in my case it was. One day toward the end of 1938, as I was lying in bed recovering from an attack and listening to Paul, my youngest son, improvising on the piano, the words of "He Rose Triumphantly" sang themselves to the metre of his music.

In 1944 B. D. Ackley asked me for a hymn on the resurrection with no mention of Easter, so that it could be sung the year around. I revised this poem which had been written to Paul's music and sent it to him. The dramatic setting that he gave it immediately made it popular.

Dr. Rodeheaver had this to say about "He Rose Triumphantly": "I believe that song will live throughout the centuries and will give many thousands of people a new vision of what the Resurrection means to the world."

"I WILL TRUST"

One day during the war, July 14th, 1944, when I was preaching in Detroit, I received a telegram stating that my youngest son, Paul, who was studying for the ministry, had been called up. I was stunned for I had thought that he was exempt, and I knew that the Lord had called him to preach. In my despair I cried mightily to God and at last heard Him whisper, "I will trust." Then I began to write, and in a few minutes I had a new hymn to which B. D. Ackley wrote the music. Later it was discovered that a mistake had been made, so the order was rescinded, and Paul was free to follow the call of God.

"THE FINEST OF THE WHEAT"

I wrote "The Finest of the Wheat" in my room at McCormick Theological Seminary, Chicago, on April 4th, 1913, when I was 23. It was the outcome of my great disappointment and sorrow. I kept it until 1946, when I sent it to B. D. Ackley, who then wrote the beautiful setting to which it is now sung.

"FORGIVE ME FOR FORGETTING"

One day when I was at Winona Lake, Dr. Homer Rodeheaver showed me a new musical composition, and asked me to write words for it. He told me that just as he was getting into his berth on the train one night, he suddenly remembered that he had not said his prayers. Immediately he cried, "O Lord, forgive me for forgetting!" Later he wrote the music with that thought in mind.

Well, I worked over it for a long time. My first attempt was unsatisfactory. A year later, July 31st, 1948, while in Toronto, I tried again, and this time my poem was accepted. Dr. Rodeheaver sang it, told the story and preached a sermon with each verse.

"A CROWN OF GLORY"

In the year 1911 Jennie M. Tyrrell composed and sent me a short poem. In 1958 I read it again and I was impressed by the first verse which I felt led to use. I then wrote the chorus and the three other verses. A few days later she died and so she never saw it published. I then sent it to B. D. Ackley and he immediately wrote the lovely music to which it is now sung.

It was his last composition, for he wrote it just before he died. What a fitting memorial!

ACKLEY'S PREDICTIONS

It is interesting to note B. D. Ackley's various predictions in connection with these hymns at the time they first appeared. I leave others to judge as to whether or not they have been fulfilled.

For instance, in connection with "Joy in Serving Jesus," Mr. Ackley had this to say on July 31st, 1930: "I know it is a winner. A writer usually has a 'hunch' when he writes something that he knows positively will go over." On January 22nd, 1932, he said this: " 'Joy in Serving Jesus' is going over big. Hall-Mack Company suggest that I get another with as much 'pep' and such a message."

Regarding "The Saviour Can Solve Every Problem," he wrote as follows on May 27th, 1932: "I have not yet had a plate made for the best of all the poems you have sent me. I mean 'best,' because it is going to be the most useful when it once gets a start. 'The Saviour Can Solve Every Problem' will be the 'star' of all the songs I have written in the past five years."

On November 7th, 1932, he wrote: " 'Satisfied With Thee' is the best of anything I have done from a musical standpoint for many a moon."

In connection with "A Revival Hymn," he wrote this in 1933: "I believe we've got a real winner here, one that you will hear from in a large way. It is an up-to-date song that has a live message for this day, and I believe it is going to find its way around the world before its popularity wanes."

About "Where Dreams Come True," in 1935, he wrote: "I am sure that in this poem you have a song that will be heard from. Dr. Rodeheaver is singing it everywhere he goes and it is taking fire. It is sure to become a favourite."

In speaking about "The Glory of His Presence," on July 13th, 1935, he wrote: "This song is bound to become popular."

In connection with "God Understands," on November 16th, 1938, he had this to say: " 'God Understands' is meeting a most favourable response and is increasing in popularity all the time." On February 10th, 1940, he wrote this: "Rody is using your 'God Understands' everywhere he goes and folks like it. I believe it is going to become very popular as a solo."

Regarding "The Broken Threads of Life," he wrote on November 16th, 1938, as follows: "I believe this is the best number I have written since 'God Understands'."

His word about "Pray On," on November 17th, 1938, is worth quoting: "It is one of the finest two-brace songs written in many years. It strikes immediate response wherever used."

In reference to "Then Jesus Came," on May 28th, 1940, he said: " 'Then Jesus Came' is going over big. Rody uses it at every service as our closing number and follows it with an invitation of some sort."

Regarding "With Thy Spirit Fill Me," on August 21st, 1940, he wrote: "We are using 'With Thy Spirit Fill Me' at each service. Everyone already is familiar with the melody. It makes a most appropriate number just before a preaching service. Rody sometimes has the crowd, as they sit down just before the sermon, hum it softly, and the effect is marvellous. I believe you and I have collaborated on something in this song that will carry along many years after we have both passed over to the other side."

About "Be Thou Near," on March 16th, 1944, he wrote: " 'Be Thou Near' is bound to live after all of us are gone."

HIS APPRECIATION

It is also interesting to recall Mr. Ackley's gracious comments in regard to our collaboration.

On April 6th, 1932, he wrote: "I want you to know how much I have appreciated your work. It takes time for a poet and a song writer to understand each other. Your poems are of a type that appeal more and more to me."

On August 5th, 1935, he wrote: "You are going to be much better known as a Writer of Poems within the next few months than in any of the years that have gone before."

On January 29th, 1936, he wrote: "I have been able to grasp your thought expressed in your poems, and, between us, we have made a happy union, and one that I believe will continue after we have both passed to the other side."

On September 25th, 1940, he wrote: "I have deeply appreciated your spirit through the years in furnishing me with your lyrics. Our work together seems to have been quite successful and I believe that our songs, where you have written the words, will be sung more and more."

Complete stories of 48 of my best known hymns have now been published by The Rodeheaver Co., along with the hymns themselves, both words and music, in an attractive book.

SOME OF THE SECRETS

Hymns, like people, have to be well married to really live. To B. D. Ackley I owe a debt of gratitude that I will never be able to repay, for he had such a gift of melody that the music fits the words as though the two had been born together. We collaborated for 28 years. He died on September 3rd, 1958.

Then, too, much credit must be given to The Rodeheaver Co. for the popularization of these hymns, for were it not for them, many of them would never have become known. But they have put them in their books and thus introduced them to multiplied thousands. Many of them are on victrola records.

It has been a great joy to know and correspond with the noted hymn-writers of the day. I have entertained George C. Stebbins, Robert Harkness, Homer Rodeheaver and B. D. Ackley in my home. I knew D. B. Towner personally. I still have a letter which I prize very highly, that I received from Fanny Crosby, the blind hymn-writer. Billy Sunday's famous Song-Leader, Homer Rodeheaver, and Billy Graham's Leader, Cliff Barrows, have both led the singing in my meetings.

Poets, they say, are born, not made. Well, perhaps so. Be that as it may, the gift, I know, has to be developed. When I was in my early twenties I purchased volumes of poetry and read the poems aloud so as to get what is called "rhythm" into my soul. Such works as Milton's "Paradise Lost" and Dante's "Inferno" I read line by line aloud. Tennyson, Browning, Byron, Bryant, Longfellow, Hood, Whittier, Shakespeare, and a whole shelf of others, I literally devoured. These volumes I still have, and they are marked throughout. While I was in Chicago I conducted a class in the study of Tennyson, my favourite poet.

J. Edwin Orr, Th.D., D.Phil. (Oxon), wrote: "Oswald Smith's 1,200 hymns, poems and gospel songs have made him Canada's best known and most prolific hymn writer. Not only so, but his hymns have more spiritual depth than most contemporary productions, and they excel in quality of word and music the popular songs of the Nineteenth Century. I remember Peter Marshall, beloved chaplain of the United States Senate, telling me how he was first attracted to Oswald Smith by his hymns."

George C. Stebbins, world famous composer in D. L. Moody's day, and my personal friend, had this to say about my hymns: "Dr. Smith has played upon a harp of many strings, touching the varied experiences of men in a winsome and appealing way. His songs will bring hope to the sinner weary with his sin, and joy and comfort to God's children on their homeward way."

CHAPTER XIII

THE PRESENT OUTLOOK

Now let me gather up the fragments that remain. And first of all a word about a work that to me is as important as my preaching. I refer to my literary endeavours. The pen is mightier than the voice. My ministry, I feel sure, will be carried on by what I have written long after I am gone.

BOOKS

Down through the years God has permitted me to write and publish 35 books, and these have had a combined circulation of 3 million copies. They have been sent to thousands of missionaries throughout the world, and have been a source of spiritual blessing and salvation everywhere.

I started by writing tracts, and later, at my own expense, I got them out, then used them as chapters and published them in book form. Finally The Christian and Missionary Alliance of New York took over the publishing of my books. Now they are published, for the most part, by Marshall, Morgan & Scott of London, England. A few have been issued by The Moody Press, the Zondervan Publishing House and the Van Kampen Press.

During the days of Mussolini I published a number of my prophetic messages in a book called, *Is The Antichrist At Hand?* It sold out almost overnight. So great was the interest created that the Christian and Missionary Alliance sent their representative from New York to obtain the publication rights. Within a very short time something like one hundred thousand copies had been sold and I found myself in great demand as a preacher on prophecy at 35 years of age.

Within the last five years I have been revising my books and now I have reduced them from 35 to 14 volumes, retaining only the vital and permanent messages and omitting much material of a temporary and local nature. So far as possible I now have one book for each subject. They have been translated into more than 60 different languages and are distributed worldwide. Several now have many more pages.

Following are the titles of this library of 14 volumes that now constitute the legacy that I will leave, all published by Marshall, Morgan and Scott, to whom I owe a debt of gratitude. They have sold over 735,000 copies.

The Country I Love Best	The Story of My Life
The Marvels of Grace	The Lives of Brainerd and
The Man God Uses	Fletcher
The Enduement of Power	Tales of the Mission Field
The Passion for Souls	The Adventures of Andy
The Cry of the World	McGinnis
Prophecy—What Lies Ahead?	The Stories of Thomas
The Challenge of Life	Poems of a Lifetime

All over Australia, New Zealand, South Africa, North America, Great Britain, and the mission fields of the world these books are well known and much has been written about them. Rev. Jack McAlister, Founder and Director of World Literature Crusade, with whom I have co-operated in Radio Missionary Conventions, has helped tremendously in the distribution of my books both in English and many other languages.

My friend, Dr. J. Edwin Orr, once wrote a most interesting sketch of my life and ministry in a book entitled "Always Abounding."

DEGREES

On May 31st, 1936, I was given the degree of Doctor of Divinity by Asbury Seminary. On May 8th, 1939, I was made a Life Member of the Royal Geographical Society of London. On May 29th, 1940, I received my Doctor of Literature degree from Bob Jones University. On September 30th, 1940, I was made a member of the Eugene Field Society. On June 3rd, 1946, the degree of Doctor of Laws was conferred upon me by Houghton College. On January 1st, 1952, I was made a Member of the Royal Society of Literature of the United Kingdom. On December 24th, 1953, I became a Member of the American Society of Composers and Authors.

HOBBIES AND FRIENDS

About my only hobbies have been photography, ornithology and paintings.

My files are filled with letters from many well-known people with whom I have carried on a correspondence—Sir Wilfred Grenfell, General Sir Arthur Smith, Chas. M. Alexander, G. Campbell Morgan, F. B. Meyer, Christabel Pankhurst, Mrs. "Ma" Sunday, Mrs. R. A. Torrey, Gipsy Smith, Wm. E. Blackstone, Billy Graham, Evan Roberts, Homer Rodeheaver, Robt. Harkness, Peter Bilhorn, Premier E. C. Manning, Geo. C. Stebbins, Fanny Crosby, Dr. Griffith Thomas, Paul Rader, D. M. Panton, and many others.

SERMONS

I have now, 1966, preached over 11,000 sermons and I have a record of every one, from the time I stood in the pulpit of the Severn Church when I was eighteen, until today. I cannot speak of thousands of converts as some can, but I have seen many walk down the aisles, and I have reason to believe that God has used my messages to the salvation of some at least. To Him be the glory. The Day will declare it.

I have married more than 500 couples and have dedicated hundreds of babies.

FAMILY

It may be of interest to know that our eldest son, Glen Gilmour Smith, B.A., M.D., F.R.C.S., is now a specialist in Vancouver. I married him to Kathleen Olive Powers on May 27th, 1944. They have three children, a girl and two boys. Glen plays the piano. He is a skilled surgeon.

Hope Evangeline, our one and only daughter, I married to Captain Donovan Lowry on August 17th, 1940. They have three children, two boys and a girl. Don is a Trans-Canada Air Pilot. Hope is an author, a poet and an artist.

Our youngest son, Rev. Paul Brainerd Smith, B.A., D.D., F.R.G.S., the Associate Pastor of The Peoples Church since September 1st, 1952, became Pastor on January 1st, 1959. For several years he did evangelistic work in Canada, Great Britain, the West Indies, New Zealand, Australia, the Orient, South Africa, and the United States. He is a gifted preacher, expositor and soul-winner. I married him to Anita Lawson on

June 8th, 1946. They have three children, a boy and two girls. Paul has written 7 major volumes, "Church Aflame", "After Midnight", "Naked Truth", "World Conquest", "Headline Pulpit", "Daily Gospel" and "Perilous Times".

My dear father went Home to be with the Lord on May 24th, 1955. It was the first break in our family since the death of my eldest sister, Hazel, in fifty years. Although he was 92, he looked years younger for there was not a wrinkle in his face. He was an aristocrat of the old school. Ernie and I took the funeral service, and we buried him at Embro beside Hazel. The last thing he said to me was, "I want you to know that I am the Lord's." What a comfort to my heart.

My darling little Mother went Home to be with Christ on May 5th, 1958, when she was 89 years of age. She died in my home and she was conscious to the last. The funeral service was conducted by Rev. Robt. Watt in The Peoples Church. She was buried beside Father and Hazel in the Embro Cemetery. Her six sons attended. It was a terrific ordeal. I loved my parents and they had a great love for me.

Chrissie French, who helped raise our children, is still with us, and she is now raising our grand-children. All our children were saved in their childhood days. All are active for God. In 1953 and 1960 I was in the hospital for surgical operations.

"No good thing will He withhold from them that walk up-rightly." How true that has been. Each move has been a move north. I used to live at 2 Bruce. When we were married we started life at 58 Garden. Next 242 Gladstone. Then 6 Muir. After that 716 Palmerston. Next 22 Kendal. From there we moved to 15 Conrad. Then 46 Buckingham. Now 31 Berkindale Drive. How good God has been.

ANNIVERSARIES

On March 27th, 1955, we celebrated my Twenty-fifth Anniversary as Pastor of The Peoples Church. All the newspapers published wonderful reports with pictures. Letters and telegrams poured in, one from Hon. George Drew, Leader of the Opposition in Ottawa. Gordon Sinclair gave a marvellous radio commentary. *The Star Weekly* gave a full page with pictures. This was from the year we moved to Gerrard St.

The auditorium was crowded, so was the vestibule, aisles and steps, and there were many turned away. I told the story of my Call to Toronto and of the founding of The Peoples Church, as already recorded. The people listened breathlessly. There was great enthusiasm and souls were saved.

Mrs. Smith and I were presented with a love-offering of some $1,500 from the Congregation and a beautiful leather-bound Address; and from the Elders a Sterling Silver Tea Service. There was an atmosphere of unity, love and appreciation, that will never be forgotten. We used our love-offering to help pay our expenses to Africa.

On May 18th, 1958, I celebrated the Golden Jubilee of my ministry, 1908 to 1958—fifty years of preaching. The service was held on Sunday night in the great Varsity Arena, seating 6,000. We had a Choir of 500 voices. All the children took part. My wife was presented with 50 yellow roses and we were given a new Buick car. A beautiful Jubilee Record, with greetings from Billy Graham and a number of my songs, was produced by Walt. Huntley and widely distributed. Souls were saved. God was glorified. The newspapers gave glowing accounts.

On January 1st, 1959, at 69 years of age, I became Minister of Missions of The Peoples Church, and the Board appointed my youngest son Paul, 37, Pastor. I continue to occupy the pulpit with him and I am in charge when he is absent. I can now give more time to The Peoples Missionary Society, of which I am President, and I will be able to respond to some of the many invitations I am receiving from foreign lands. I am still Editor of The Peoples Magazine and Manager of the Book Department. These have been 40 glorious years in The Peoples Church but I believe its greatest days are still ahead. Thanks be unto God.

I would like to say that Frank Trenchard, who has been our organist for 25 years, and Donald Billings, our brilliant pianist, who has been with us since the beginning of the work, have been a tremendous inspiration and help.

David E. Williams, B.A., became our Minister of Music on October 1st, 1960. He is a gifted composer, song leader and choir director. On January 1st, 1967, Miss Norma Cooper became Minister of Education.

On June 5th, 1961, The Peoples Church was sold for $650,000. We paid $75,000. In 1962 a new church was built under the leadership of the Pastor, Dr. Paul B. Smith at 374 Sheppard Avenue East, eight miles north on 5 acres of land, accommodating 2,500 people. Thus, after giving almost everything to Missions (5 million dollars) for 34 years, God has given us a new church free of debt with plenty of parking space and all the rooms we need for our work. How like Him! The ground was broken on November 12th, 1961, in the presence of some 3,000 people, and the corner stone was laid on June 3rd, 1962. It was opened on October 28th, 1962, with three great services, attended by some 7,000 people, debt free. The vision has now been fulfilled.

CONCLUSION

As I look back over the years of my life and ministry, I can only exclaim "What hath God wrought!" How faithful He has been. Truly I am not worthy of the least of His mercies. God definitely called me to found a great evangelistic, soul-winning, missionary work, in Toronto. He called me the first time from Chicago, when I was in my twenties, and gave me Dale Presbyterian Church. I stayed three-and-a-half years and then, like Jonah, I ran away 3,000 miles to British Columbia. He called me the second time from British Columbia in my thirties and gave me The Alliance Tabernacle. I stayed five-and-a-half years and then ran away again 3,000 miles to California. He called me a third time all the way from California and gave me The Peoples Church. This time I stayed for some 40 years and saw the vision fulfilled. I feel that I can now say: "I have finished the work which Thou gavest me to do."

To think that The Peoples Church has the largest regular Sunday evening attendance of any church in the whole of Canada, and that it is now world famous, is nothing short of miraculous. But, more wonderful still—God chose a boy from a country railway station to bring it into existence. This is the Lord's doing, and it is marvellous in my eyes.

Whether or not I made a mistake when I left Dale or when I resigned from The Alliance Tabernacle, only God knows. Many things would have been different had I stayed. Very seldom does a minister succeed when he returns to his former field of service. Yet twice God has brought me back. It humbles me to the dust as I think of it. How undeserving I have been! And He has been so good to me. Body, soul and spirit, I am His. Yes, His for all Eternity. To know Him and to make Him known is now my one and only object in life.

No great work has ever been accomplished without much suffering. Great success is always followed by great conflict and testing. Those who have been used of God have had to pay a terrific price. Much of my prayer life has been characterized by humiliation and confession. But though I have often failed Him, He has never failed me, nor have I ever been tempted to turn back. However, I wish I had been more devoted and more faithful to my Lord.

As I look back over my life I feel that my wife has made the greatest sacrifice. She it was who stayed at home to look after the children while I was away touring the world for five and six months at a time and, because she did, they are what they are today. No one will ever know how lonely she was as she held the ropes that I might go. Her sufferings were intense, for she has never been well. All through life she has stood loyally with me. Her love has never failed. Only God, who saw her tears, can reward her for the sacrifices she made. I could never have accomplished what I have had it not been for her. I owe her more than I can ever pay.

Our dear Chrissie, who lived with us for 41 years, went Home to be with Christ on January 20th 1964. Oh, how we miss her! She was a great prayer-warrior.

On September 12th, 1966, we celebrated our Golden Wedding with a public reception in our home and 2,200 people in the church. There were 18 decisions for Christ. Letters, cards, and cables came from all over the world, the Governor-General of Canada, the Prime Minister, Billy Graham, and more than a thousand others who contacted us. How good God has been!

Every few years I get in my car and motor back to where the old Embro Station once stood, and alone I walk the ties and paths I walked so long ago. Slowly I cross the fields or stand and meditate under the old trees, the trees I climbed when a barefoot boy. I never want to forget the pit out of which I was digged. It humbles me to go back to the scenes of the past.

How glad I am that He called me and that I was not disobedient to the heavenly vision. The future is all His. Today I am more eager than ever to burn out for God, and to see once again a manifestation of His power.